LOVE LETTERS FROM JOHN

LOVE LETTERS FROM JOHN

A DEVOTIONAL COMMENTARY ON THE EPISTLES OF JOHN

DR. GEORGE R. CARMAN

ISBN-10: 1944704310
ISBN-13: 978-1944704315

Published by Start2Finish
Fort Worth, Texas 76244
www.start2finish.org

Printed in the United States of America

Cover Design: Josh Feit, Evangela.com

CONTENTS

DEDICATION

This book is lovingly dedicated to my wife, Hilda Carman. She has been my companion for over 51 years and is a faithful servant of God most high. She is a very capable teacher of Children's Bible classes. The Epistles of John are among her favorites. I lovingly dedicate this volume to the love of my life.

ACKNOWLEDGEMENT

I want to express my sincere appreciation to my sister, Karen Jinkerson, for her excellent proofreading of this manuscript. She graciously volunteered her time to pour over this book looking for sentence structure and continuity of thought. This commentary has been made much better because of her diligent help and suggestions.

PRELIMINARY CONSIDERATIONS

Before beginning our study of the Epistles of John I wanted to provide you with a special study to assist you in your quest for Bible knowledge. This information is a compilation of information I have gleaned over the years that has been of tremendous help to me personally as I have studied the Scriptures. Look it over and see if you can reap some helpful information on how to go deeper into the word of God.

SPECIAL STUDY ON BIBLE STUDY

Far too many people find the Bible too confusing for them to understand. The Eunuch from Acts 8:26-40 is a prime example. He was very interested in serving the Lord and in studying the Bible. As we read about his conversion we learn he was on his way home from a trip to Jerusalem. As he traveled he was reading from Isaiah 53, a passage that spoke of the coming of the Christ. Philip, the evangelist, asked the Eunuch if he understood what he was reading. His response was "How can I unless someone guides me?" (Acts 8:31). Don't we all sometimes feel a lack of understanding when we pour over the word of God? The following Bible study suggestions should make it easier for you to come to a better understanding of the word of God.

THE BIBLE CLAIMS TO BE THE WORD OF GOD: If you will take the time to look at the 12 Minor Prophets you will see that the human authors often informed their audience that their message came from God. "Thus says the Lord" is a popular phrase found in the twelve Minor Prophets. The claim to be from God is found throughout the Old Testament. One unknown author gave a list of the books in the Old Testament noting that they claimed to be from God 3,808 times. If the Bible did not come from God it is a fraud. If it did come through Divine sources we should carefully and prayerfully study and meditate upon its words.

THE BIBLE IS THE WORD OF GOD: All scripture is God breathed (inspired) of God (2 Timothy 3:16-17). Thus it is not quite accurate to say the Bible contains the word of God. It is better to say the Bible *is* the word of God. "Knowing this first of all, that no prophecy of Scripture comes from someone's own interpretation. 21For no prophecy was ever produced by the will of man, but men spoke from God as they were carried along by the Holy Spirit" (2 Pet. 1:20-21).

Therefore, every word found in the original text of the Bible is inspired of God. It is of vital importance that Bible students understand this truth. If the Bible is not inspired it becomes just another religious book making bogus claims that it came from God to man. An uninspired Bible is of little value to us except as one more ancient book from the past. However, if the Bible is inspired of God, then everything in it is vitally important for us to study, to learn, and to accept as truth. We must also obey its commandments.

CHARACTERISTICS OF A GOOD BIBLE STUDENT

1. He has complete faith that the Bible is the inspired, infallible word of God (2 Tim. 3:16-17).
2. He has pure motives. He wants only to learn and understand the word

of God. He seeks knowledge for the purpose of finding the will of God (Eph. 5:17).

3. He prays without ceasing (1 Thess. 5:17).
4. He has a strong desire to learn more (1 Pet. 2:1-2; 2 Pet. 3:18; Psa. 19:7-11).
5. He desires to know, and to understand scripture. For him the word is sweet as honey to his taste (Psa. 119:97-104).
6. He has the courage to change his understanding based upon the teachings found in Scripture (Acts 18:24-28). Apollos' understanding of the word of God changed because of Bible study.
7. A good bible student never forgets that God's word is truth (John 17:17). Therefore, he embraces the idea of a lifetime pursuit of the divine truths found in Scripture.
8. His love for God is so great that he cannot but obey the commandments found in the Bible (1 John 5:1-5).

FUNDAMENTAL APPROACH TO STUDY

To be successful in learning the Bible one must have a sound approach to learning. He must love reading and studying the Bible. Reading and studying are not the same things. We need to do both. I suggest you read the entire Bible all the way through each and every year. This is *not* Bible study but it serves to give you communion with the word of God and it keeps the word fresh in your mind. After all, when you read the Bible God is talking to you. When you study you are putting the word of God into your heart. When we read and study then the word becomes available for us to use in times of need.

Be inquisitive as you study from the Bible. Learn the eight fundamentals for Bible study listed below. Be like a newspaper reporter and ask yourself the following questions:

Who was the human author? While this is wonderful information you must never forget the human author was not writing his own words. He wrote inspired words that were given to him by the Holy Spirit.

To whom was the book written? Knowing the recipient is important because it gives us background information that will assist us in understanding the book. In many cases we can learn more about the recipients by searching other verses in the Bible that mention them. This helps us to round out our understanding.

What is the purpose of the book? This is an essential ingredient for understanding the book. First of all, look at the background of the book. For example, when you study 1 Corinthians you will discover that Paul wrote the book to correct some problems that had infiltrated the church. Paul wrote to help them get back on the right track.

What did the book mean to the recipients and what does it mean to me? After determining what the book meant to the original recipients we must make an application of the lessons to ourselves. It is important to learn what the text means to me today. Are there commandments to obey? Are there examples to follow? Ask yourself the question, "How can I use this information to grow in the Lord"?

When was the book written? This information varies from scholar to scholar. However, it is good to get a sense of when the book you are studying was written.

Always consider the context of the passage you are studying. You must read the verse(s) before and after the section you are studying in order to learn more about the context of the verses you are examining. Context is vital to correct understanding. If one takes a verse by itself without considering context he could easily come to a wrong conclusion. You must also consider other passages that speak to the same subject. The Psalmist said, "The sum of your word is truth" (Psa. 119:160).

Never interpret scripture in a way that contradicts other passages of

scripture. When your interpretation conflicts with other clear and plain passages of scripture, then your understanding is incorrect. God does not contradict Himself. It is good to research other passages that deal with the same topic. Doing so will broaden your understanding of the portion of Scripture that you are currently studying.

Know that you can understand Scripture. It might take years, or even a lifetime, but you can learn and understand the Bible. Be patient. Over time you will learn the word of God. When you study correctly you will transform your mind to become more like the mind of Jesus (Rom. 12:1-2). You will also become a shining light to others as you live out the messages you learn from God's holy word in your daily life. "Your word is a lamp to my feet and a light to my path" (Psalms 119:105). When you walk in the truth you become an example that others can follow as you follow Christ (1 Cor. 11:1).

Try to make in-depth Bible study a regular part of your life. It will enrich your faith and it will help you to remain steadfast in your Christian walk. Be assured, God will bless your efforts

CHAPTER ONE

INTRODUCTION

We are about to embark upon a fascinating journey into the inspired Epistles of the apostle John. The apostle will present his eyewitness account of Jesus Christ, the Son of God. In addition to proving the Deity of Christ, we will learn of fellowship, walking in the light, the forgiveness of sins, and the love of God. John will also address the false religious teachers of his day. He calls them antichrists because they denied that Jesus was the Son of God. They also denied that Jesus came in the flesh thereby denying the truth that Jesus was God made flesh.

John also addresses other important lessons that will strengthen our faith. We will learn the necessity of testing the messages we receive from our teachers so that we can determine whether the teaching is true or false. He speaks of the necessity of obeying God's commandments. The book of Second John will challenge us to walk according to the commandments and to refuse to have fellowship with false teachers. "Do not receive him into your house or give him any greeting" (2 John 10). Third John teaches the necessity of financially supporting traveling evangelists. We also learn about a church leader named Diotrephes, a leader who overstepped his authority and abused his leadership position. All of these meaningful topics, and more, will be discovered as we study the 133 verses that make up the three Epistles of John.

LOVE IS A DOMINANT THEME

"By this we know love, that he laid down his life for us, and we ought to lay down our lives for the brothers" (1 John 3:16).

Take a few minutes and read the verses that contain the word "love" that are listed below. It won't take long and it will give you a flavor of the good lessons that are yet to come:

THE WORD *LOVE* IN THE EPISTLES OF JOHN

CHAPTER	VERSES	TOTAL
CHAPTER 1	0	0
CHAPTER 2	5, 10, 15	5
CHAPTER 3	1, 10, 11, 14, 16-18, 23	9
CHAPTER 4	7-12, 16-21	27
CHAPTER 5	1-3	5
2 JOHN	1, 3, 5, 6	4
3 JOHN	1, 6	2

TOTAL: 52

John's epistles present the topic of love in many helpful ways. One of the most significant teachings is the powerful statement, "God is love" (1 John 4:8). This informs us that it is not just that God loves, even though He truly does. Here we learn that God *is* love. Love is the essence of His being. Little babies receive love and eventually learn to love their family members and others. There are probably some people who achieve a very high level of Godlike love but no one can say, "I am love." That level is found only in Deity. The great emphasis these epistles place upon love provided me with the title for this commentary: "Love Letters from John."

THE DEITY OF CHRIST

The epistles of John provide compelling evidence that confirms the Deity of Jesus Christ. This topic is of central importance to John as he fights against an emerging gnostic doctrine. Gnosticism was not fully developed, however, it was in its early stages. These people claimed to have special knowledge and were eroding the faith of many believers by teaching a false doctrine on the Deity of Christ. John stood in opposition to those teachers whom he called antichrists. We will explore that false teaching as we progress in our study.

THE GNOSTIC PROBLEM

Gnosticism comes from the Greek word "ginosko," meaning: "to perceive, observe, obtain a knowledge of or insight into." It denotes a personal and true relation between the person knowing and the object known." The teaching called Gnosticism slowly developed over a period of many years. During John's day it was a doctrine in its early stages of development. Basically, the gnostic teacher of John's day denied that Jesus came in the flesh and they also denied that Jesus was the Son of God.

Gnostic teachers claimed to have special knowledge that others did not have. They taught that common folks could only learn the deeper things of God from people with "special knowledge." The truth is, the word of God was written so that *all men* could receive saving faith through studying and through an understanding of the word of God. Peter clearly stated that we "ordinary" Christians have "obtained a faith of equal standing with ours" (2 Pet. 1:1). Therefore, whether it is an Apostle, or a preacher, or an elder, or anyone else, we can all achieve the same kind of faith that dwelt in Peter and other faithful church leaders. This faith comes by hearing the word of God (Rom. 10:17).

BASIC BELIEFS OF GNOSTICISM

Early in the first century a group of early Christians began to develop teachings that came to be called Gnosticism. The teachers were called Gnostics meaning, "to know." Most Gnostics came to believe that God is good and man (and matter) is evil. They are unable to comprehend how God (who is good) could become a man (who is evil). To them good and evil cannot co-exist. Therefore they rejected the idea that Jesus was both God and man. Below are some Gnostic beliefs that developed over the passing of time.

Emanation: These Gnostics taught that the great God, who is totally good, was too holy to deal directly with mankind. The theory of emanation came out of this false concept. This theory says many lesser Gods emanated from a great and holy God. The emanated Gods were not as good nor were they as holy as the great and flawless God.

They believed that one of these lesser Gods was Jehovah, the God who created the world in which we live. The Bible does not support this idea at all. The God of the Bible, Jehovah, said, "I am the first and the last; besides me there is no god" (Isa. 44:6). He also said, "Is there a God besides me? There is no Rock; I know not any" (Isa. 44:8). There are *no* lesser gods.

Evil: The Gnostics claimed that the God who created the world was imperfect. Therefore, He created a flawed world. This doctrine is incompatible with the creation account found in Genesis chapters one and two. After most of the days of creation God said, "It is good." This does not sound like a lesser God who created an imperfect world does it? For sure, God's creation was good – not evil. After day six "God saw everything that he had made, and behold, it was very good" (Gen. 1:31). This statement completely rejects the idea that God created an imperfect world. Matter is *not evil*!

Man is evil: The Gnostic also believed that man, being fleshly, is evil from his birth. However, they believed sinful man can be given a divine spirit. There is no doubt that the time will come when all men will sin (Rom. 3:23). However, when

God created the world He looked at man and everything else He had made and said, "It is very good." Man is born sinless and pure. God gave mankind the ability to choose between good and evil. We call this free will. It is only after a person grows to understand the difference between good and evil that he commits sin. We sin because we are tempted and because we often make bad choices.

Newborn babies and little children are not sinful at all. Jesus said, "Let the little children come to me and do not hinder them, for to such belongs the kingdom of heaven" (Matt. 19:14). The Greek word for little children is "paidion" meaning "a little child, an infant." If infants belong to the kingdom of heaven they are certainly not sinners! Ezekiel wrote, "The soul who sins shall die. The son shall not suffer for the iniquity of the father, nor the father suffer for the iniquity of the son" (Ezek. 18:20). Evil does not come from God but from satan and his angels. A person sins when he falls to temptation and makes wrong choices. No one is born a sinner.

Jesus was not divine: The Gnostics of John's day denied the deity of Christ. They denied that Jesus was God made flesh. They believed that He only appeared to be a man but was really not human. "For many deceivers have gone out into the world, those who do not confess the coming of Jesus Christ in the flesh. Such a one is the deceiver and the antichrist" (2 John 7). When Jesus called Himself the Son of God His listeners knew He was claiming to be God (John 5:18).

Jesus came in the flesh and Christ is divine: Another Gnostic error was the assertion that Jesus was the ordinary son of Joseph and Mary. In other words, he was born of fleshly parents having both a mother and father just like the rest of us. This led to the false teaching that when Jesus was baptized the Divine Christ entered into the fleshly man Jesus. This Gnostic theory claims that when Jesus died on the cross Christ left him and He once again became an ordinary human being. They came to this conclusion because they believed that God could not have died upon the cross because God is eternal. A study of scripture shows us that Jesus was born of Mary by a miracle of God. Joseph had no part in Mary conceiving a son. Jesus is both God, as expressed in John 1:1-3, and man, as stated in Matthew 1:18-23. "A virgin shall conceive and bear a son" (Matt. 1:23). The Apostle

John adds his testimony to that of the other inspired writers.

Sin is ignorance: Many Gnostics believe that sin comes into our lives because of ignorance. Therefore, if we can gain enough knowledge we can overcome sin. If this is true, why do we need a Savior? Why not just overcome our sins by gaining "great" knowledge? There is no doubt that a lack of knowledge will lead men into sin (Hos. 4:6). However, knowledge by itself cannot bring us to the point where we no longer sin. "If we say we have no sin, we deceive ourselves, and the truth is not in us" (1 John 1:8). We will study the topic of sin in the chapters to follow.

Special Knowledge: As we have noted, the Gnostic claimed special knowledge. For others to gain this knowledge they must go to those who had been blessed in a special way. However, Jesus said, "You will know the truth and the truth will set you free" (John 8:32). "Sanctify them in the truth, your word is truth" (John 17:17). Knowledgeable men can certainly help us to understand the truth more clearly but these men are not the source of truth. The source of truth is found in the divinely inspired word of God – not in the uninspired words of men (2 Tim. 3:16-17). We all have the ability to learn God's will from studying Scripture.

If you cannot find the basis for your religious beliefs in the word of God, your beliefs are not essential to salvation. If the Bible teaches something different from what you believe you must discard your error and follow the plain and clear teachings that are found in the Bible. The Bible is more than adequate to lead us into all truth (John 8:32).

AUTHOR: JOHN THE SON OF ZEBEDEE

The New Testament gives us a good deal of information on John the son of Zebedee and Salome, his mother. Many believe that a comparison of Matthew 27:56 to Mark 16:1 helps to identify the name of John's mother as Salome. Many scholars also believe she was the sister of Mary, the mother of Jesus. These ideas about John's mother may be true but we cannot know with absolute certainty.

When John met Jesus he was a fisherman by trade. Even though their names are not mentioned, it is possible that James and John met Jesus for the first time while they were in Judea (John 1:29-51). James and John worked as Galilean fishermen with their father, Zebedee. Simon Peter was a partner in their fishing business. Jesus found Peter and Andrew fishing in the Sea of Galilee on the same day the Lord called James and John to follow Him (Luke 5:10; Matt. 4:18). Jesus promised to make them fishers of men (Mark 1:16-20). You might want to search out all of the New Testament passages that speak of John. There is much to learn about this great man of God.

JOHN'S WEAKNESSES

It is very important to realize that the Bible does not gloss over the weaknesses of His servants. Had uninspired men written the accounts of these honorable men they probably would have left out some of the stories that showed the flaws and sins they committed. However, all the writers of the Bible wrote by the inspiration of the Holy Spirit and they recorded the exact information on each person and each event exactly as God revealed it to them. They wrote the good and the bad. Below are two of the weaknesses found in the life of the Apostle John.

AN ANGRY YOUNG MAN: John and his brother James were both men who were quick to anger. This trait won them the nickname "Boanerges" which means "sons of thunder" (Mark 3:17). Once, when Jesus and His disciples were passing through a town in Samaria, the people of the town refused to let Jesus and his disciples enter their town because their destination was Jerusalem. James and John, the sons of thunder asked, "Lord, do you want us to tell fire to come down from heaven and consume them? But he turned and rebuked them" (Luke 9:54-55). Later in life John seems to have overcome this weakness in his character. Isn't it encouraging to know that, with God's help, we can strengthen our areas of weakness and become better, more fruitful, servants of the Lord?

HIGHLY AMBITIOUS: In the gospels James and John are mentioned together on many occasions. Some believe that since James was mentioned first he was the predominant one of the two. However, it might be that James was listed first because he was the older brother. We really don't know. They were both overly ambitious and desired prominent positions in the Kingdom of Christ. On more than one occasion they asked Jesus to give them positions of importance in the kingdom. They asked to serve on the right and left hand of the Lord (Mark 10:35-45). This suggests that they wanted to be the number two and three persons in the hierarchy of Christ's kingdom.

In Matthew 20:20-28, their mother, Salome, made a similar request on behalf of her two sons. Of course, the other Apostles resented James and John for making these requests. They resented it because they desired those positions of prominence for themselves (Mark 10:41). Jesus pointed out that the greatest in the kingdom was the one who served (Mark 10:42-45). In God's kingdom it is not the people in high positions who are great but the lowly. It is sad that even when the Apostles met to observe the Last Supper they argued over who would be greatest in the Kingdom (Luke 22:24-27). John overcame this desire for prominence and power. In Revelation 1:1, 9 John identifies himself as "a servant, a brother, and a partner in the tribulation." Truly he did not seek preeminence. He deferred that honor to the one to whom it belonged, to the Lord Jesus Christ!

LATER EVENTS

In the gospels James and John are usually mentioned together. In the gospel of John, the Apostle never calls himself by name. Instead he uses the designation, "the disciple whom Jesus loved" (John 13:23; 21:20).

In the book of Acts we see Peter and John working together for the Lord. For an example of these two Apostles working side-by-side read Acts chapters four and five. It is not unusual that they would work as teammates. After all, they had previously been partners in a fishing business and they were both Apostles of Christ. How wonderful to see God's people working together. Peter and John had become fishers of men.

It is generally accepted that John was the only Apostle who died of natural causes. Jerome (A.D. 342-419) wrote that John lived in Ephesus towards the end of his life. He wrote that John was now so old he could not stand without help and was unable to deliver long lessons. He added that on several occasions the Apostle, while being held up by others, simply said, "Little children love one another." When asked why he kept saying the same sentence every time he spoke, John replied, "It is the Lord's command and, if this alone be done, it is enough". We do not know the accuracy of this account pertaining to John's later years but it certainly shows the love and service of an old man who still had words of encouragement to say to God's people. After a long and fruitful life, the Apostle John went on to receive His reward. Believers from the first century to the end of time will be blessed by his inspired writing.

DATE OF THE BOOKS

John wrote five New Testament books. The first was the book of Revelation, written about A.D. 76. The Gospel of John was written sometime around A.D. 85-90. The three epistles of John were written in the early to mid 90's probably from Ephesus.

INTRODUCING FIRST JOHN

A unique feature of 1 John is that the author clearly answers the question "What is the purpose for this book?" You might want to highlight John's five purpose statements in your Bible for ready reference.

JOHN'S FIVE PURPOSE STATEMENTS

1. **FIRST PURPOSE: To provide complete joy:** "That our joy may be com-

plete" (1 John 1:4). The Greek word translated "joy" means, "delight or gladness." Having joy is a good thing. Our joy comes from God and permeates our entire existence regardless of external circumstances.

2. **SECOND PURPOSE: So you may not sin:** "I am writing these things to you so that you may not sin" (1 John 2:1). While we often fall short and sin, our ultimate goal is to not sin at all. John encourages us in this holy lifestyle even though he was aware we would often fail. John provides us with information on how to handle our sin problems when they do occur. Be looking forward to more details on this topic as we get to that text.

3. **THIRD PURPOSE: Because you know the truth:** "I write to you not because you do not know the truth, but because you know it and because no lie is of the truth" (1 John 2:21). This purpose statement shows the trust the writer has in those having to deal with the false teachers. They would be successful because they knew the truth and could dispute the lies of the antichrists.

4. **FOURTH PURPOSE: So you will not be deceived:** "I write these things to you about those who are trying to deceive you" (1 John 2:26). Be aware that false teachers will attempt to deceive you with false doctrine. We must weigh any message we hear against the words of the Apostles and other inspired writers. Jeremiah warned, "Do not listen to the words of the prophets who prophesy to you, filling you with vain hopes. They speak visions of their own minds, not from the mouth of the Lord. They say continually to those who despise the word of the Lord, 'It shall be well with you'; and to everyone who stubbornly follows his own heart, they say, 'No disaster shall come upon you'" (Jer. 23:16-17). We must not allow false teachers to deceive us with false messages.

5. **FIFTH PURPOSE: So you can know you have eternal life:** "I write these things to you who believe in the name of the Son of God that you may know that you have eternal life" (1 John 5:13). Far too many believers are uncertain about the destiny of their soul. John gives us assurance that faithful believers can know that they have eternal life. Such knowledge gives us comfort and peace. All

faithful Christians should live with the certainty that they have a home in heaven. Read John 14:1-6 for further confirmation of the future home promised to the faithful.

FIVE IMPORTANT TEACHINGS

Here are five important lessons presented by John. They will be developed more fully when we get to our study of these texts.

1. The deity of Christ, the Son of God (1:1-4; 4:10, 14; 5:5).
2. The importance of walking in the light (1:5-7).
3. The reality of sin (1:8-2:1; 3:11-15).
4. The importance of love (3:1, 16, 23; 4:19-21).
5. How obedience proves our love for God and for each other (5:1-5).

JOHN'S CONCEPT OF GOD

It is interesting to learn how many of the epistles in the New Testament speak of God's nature and character. Such knowledge helps us to expand our understanding of God, our great Creator. Again, we will study the verses in greater detail later in this book.

1. God is light and in Him is no darkness at all (1 John 1:5).
2. God loved us before we loved Him (1 John 4:8, 19).
3. God manifested His love for us by sending His Son (1 John 4:9).
4. God expects our love for Him to compel us to obey His commandments, (1 John 5:2-3).

OUTLINE OF 1 JOHN

CHAPTER 1:1-2:6

1. Confirming Christ's deity (1:1-4)
2. Walking in the light (1:5-2:2)

CHAPTER 2:7-29

1. Separation from the world (2:3-17)
2. Abiding in Him (2:18-29)

CHAPTER 3:

1. Refraining from sin (3:1-10)
2. Love's compelling nature (3:11-24)

CHAPTER 4:

1. Knowing the spirit of truth (4:1-6)
2. Abide in God's love (4:7-21)

CHAPTER 5: Knowledge provides confidence (5:1-21)

DISCUSSION QUESTIONS:

1. What does it mean to you when the Bible says, "God is love"? What does the Greek word "agape" mean? Look in a lexicon or concordance.
2. What is the meaning of the word "knowledge" or "ginosko"? Is it good or is it bad to have "ginosko"? Explain 1 Corinthians 8:1 as compared to Hosea 4:6.
3. How important is it to dispute the doctrine of Gnosticism? Discuss some of the basic beliefs of this doctrine.
4. Discuss John's weaknesses. How do we overcome our own weaknesses?
5. How did Jesus reply to James and John when they requested "power" positions in the kingdom? Is it wrong to be ambitious?
6. List the five purpose statements given by John in his epistle.
7. Date the five books written by the Apostle John.

CHAPTER TWO

CONFIRMING CHRIST'S DEITY

1 JOHN 1:1-4

Now we are ready to launch into an exciting and important study on the Deity of the Christ. Doing so is always a faith building experience. There are many passages in the Bible that confirm His Deity but no study would be complete without studying the writings of the apostle John. Even though 1 John is a short epistle, it still gives us powerful testimony on this vital topic. John's explanation of the Deity of Jesus Christ is brief but it is loaded with power and clarity. The evidence that is given is undeniable.

Confirmation of Christ's Deity was necessary because of the false teaching of the antichrists. We will study the antichrists in more detail when we get to Chapter Five of this commentary. The antichrists were confusing some believers by denying that Jesus was the Son of God. They also denied that the Messiah came to earth in the flesh. The goal of the first four verses of 1 John was to bring the first-century believers to the same conclusion that was held by the inspired apostles. Here is what the apostles believed to be true concerning Jesus, "You have the words of eternal life, and we have believed, and have come to know, that you are the Holy One of God" (John 6:68-69). People in every Century can reach the same conclusion when they study God's word concerning Jesus Christ, the only begotten Son of God. Our study of 1 John 1:1-4 can help to increase our understanding and to strengthen our faith in the Deity of Jesus.

THE APOSTLES TESTIMONY

> That which was from the beginning, which we have heard, which we have seen with our eyes, which we looked upon and have touched with our hands, concerning the word of life, the life was made manifest, and we have seen it, and testify to it and proclaim to you the eternal life, which was with the Father and was made manifest to us that which we have seen and heard we proclaim also to you, so that you too may have fellowship with us; and indeed our fellowship is with the Father and with his Son Jesus Christ. And we are writing these things so that our joy may be complete.
>
> 1 John 1:1-4

The first four verses of 1 John provide us with powerful evidence that Jesus existed with God the Father from the beginning. This same Jesus came to the earth as a man. John called God the "Father" and he called Jesus "his Son." Thus the Lord was not just another child born to a Jewish family in the First Century. He had been present from the beginning. Jehovah God, Jesus, and the Holy Spirit are One and They are eternal. They worked together in creating the universe, including the world in which we live. Look at the evidence given by John. It is powerful because it comes from men who were eyewitnesses of Jesus and His ministry.

THEY HEARD THE LORD: "That which was from the beginning which we have heard" (1 John 1:1). The Apostles were eyewitnesses of Jesus and were with Him during His entire ministry. They were the eyewitnesses who heard first hand all that Jesus taught. Early in Jesus' ministry He spoke words that the crowds (and often the Apostles themselves) could not comprehend. Yet when they heard Christ teach they marveled at His knowledge and His authority.

The Sermon on the Mount was one of the Lord's greatest recorded messages (Matt. 5:1-7:29). I'm sure all of the Apostles were in awe over the lessons Jesus taught that day. The crowds who listened to the Sermon on the Mount were truly astonished at the words they heard. "And when Jesus finished these sayings, the crowds were astonished at his teaching, for he was teaching them as one who had authority, and not as their scribes" (Matt. 7:28-29).

When the Bible speaks of hearing it does not always mean our physical ears. In Matthew 13 Jesus spoke exclusively in parables. When the disciples asked him why He did so, the Lord replied, "This is why I speak to them in parables, because seeing they do not see, and hearing they do not hear, nor do they understand. Indeed in their case the prophecy of Isaiah is fulfilled that says: 'You will indeed hear but never understand'" (Matt. 13:13-14). Don't you love the children's song that says, "Be careful little ears what you hear. For the Father up above is looking down in love, so be careful little ears what you hear!"

Sometimes we cannot hear because our ears are stopped up. I have a problem with excessive earwax. When it builds up, I have to have my ears professionally cleaned. Otherwise, I hear but do not understand. When Jesus spoke to the people there were some who were spiritually dull of hearing. This prevented them from hearing. Their spiritual ears needed cleansing. Preconceived ideas, prejudice, and sin in our lives get in the way of our understanding of God's message.

Some people were taught error by well meaning people. We trust these people and as a consequence it is only with great difficulty that we accept a different explanation. Sometimes the truth is obscured because we learn it from a trusted friend or teacher. We must love the truth more than what any man teaches to us. When people constantly reject God's truth He "sends them a strong delusion, so that they may believe what is false, in order that all may be condemned who did not believe the truth but had pleasure in unrighteousness" (2 Thess. 2:11-12). Listen to the word of God with healthy ears.

The person with healthy ears not only hears the message but he understands it. The apostles heard Jesus teach over the entire course of His ministry. Their understanding grew incrementally. The result was they openly confessed their faith in Him. “We have believed and have come to know, that you are the Holy One of God” (John 6:69). When we have ears to hear we will believe what the Bible says about Jesus.

THEY SAW THE LORD: “We have seen with our eyes” (1 John 1:1). Oh what wonderful things John and the other apostles saw! They saw Jesus’ wisdom when He interacted with the Jewish leaders. They saw His compassion on those who were afflicted with various diseases. They saw Him heal the sick and cast out demons. They saw Him raise the dead. They saw Him feed the hungry multitudes. They saw Him seeking quiet time so that He could spend time praying to His Heavenly Father. During the 40 days between his resurrection and ascension they saw the risen Lord many times and they believed.

The Apostles were with the Lord for his entire ministry. Can you imagine how many miracles they saw Him perform? No doubt John marveled along with other disciples when he saw Jesus’ mighty power to heal. The Apostles were also amazed when they saw Jesus calm the stormy sea. “What sort of man is this, that even winds and sea obey him?” (Matt. 8:27). The things John saw convinced him that Jesus was not just another prophet. He was the Son of God. He proudly confessed the truth that Jesus was the Son of God. As for the crowds around Jesus, they “wondered, when they saw the mute speaking, the crippled healthy, the lame walking, and the blind seeing. And they glorified the God of Israel” (Matt. 15:31).

Surely the Apostles would never forget the day Lazarus was brought back from the dead. By the time the Lord and His disciples arrived in Bethany, Lazarus had been in the grave for four days. The process of bodily decay was already in full force. Yet Jesus brought him back to life perfectly whole (John 11:38-44)! What they saw was real. They were eyewitnesses. The apostles saw the evidence and they believed that Jesus Christ was the Son of God.

THEY LOOKED UPON THE LORD: “Which we looked upon” (1 John 1:1). To "look upon" is different than to "see." The Greek word "look upon" means to "contemplate earnestly (with the idea of desire and pleasure); to see with regard and admiration." This word carries the idea of seeing something in order to examine it. It is much more than a casual glance. Thayer says the word means to "learn by looking." For John to look upon Jesus meant he had looked beneath the surface in order to confirm the truth about His identity. He and the other Apostles made a full investigation of the facts by the process of examination. They came to know who He was.

When Jesus asked the question, "Who do people say the son of man is?" (Matt. 16:13), Peter replied with a conviction about Jesus that was held by all of the Apostles. He said, "You are the Christ, the Son of the living God" (Matt. 16:16). Peter also said of Jesus, "Being therefore exalted at the right hand of God, and having received from the Father the promise of the Holy Spirit . . . Let all the house of Israel therefore know for certain that God has made him both Lord and Christ, this Jesus whom you crucified" (Acts 2:33, 36). They looked upon the Lord and they believed He was the Son of God! When Jesus said He was the "Son of God" those who heard Him knew He was claiming equality with God (John 5:18). To look upon means to investigate thoroughly. When we do the same we will believe that Jesus is the Son of God.

THEY TOUCHED JESUS: "And have touched with our hands" (1 John 1:1). During His time on the earth the Apostles had many opportunities to physically touch Jesus. They could testify with complete confidence that Jesus was a human being and not just a spirit that looked like a man. He was the son of Mary. Jesus was a man with flesh and blood. Most authorities concede that it was John, himself, who leaned on Jesus' bosom at the Last Supper (John 13:23). Jesus was flesh and bones just like the rest of us.

When the apostles touched Jesus it provided them with sufficient proof that He was born in the flesh. Jesus did not just appear to be human. He really was born with flesh and bones. However, He was also the only Son of God (John 1:14). That distinction made Jesus a unique, one of a kind, human being. He is God's only begotten Son.

When Jesus made His first appearance to the Apostles after his resurrection from the dead Thomas was absent. Therefore, he did not believe. According to Mark 16:13, they all had a difficult time believing that Jesus really did rise from the dead. They needed proof. On His second appearance to the Apostles doubting Thomas was there. Jesus commanded him to, "Put your finger here, and see my hands, and put out your hand, and place it in my side. Do not disbelieve, but believe. Thomas answered him, 'My Lord and my God'" (John 20:27-28). Can you see how Thomas' reply is a testimony to Christ's Deity?

Jesus also appeared to several disciples by the seaside in the book of Luke. Those present thought they were seeing a spirit but Jesus said, "Why are you troubled, and why do doubts arise in your hearts? See my hands and my feet that it is I myself. Touch me and see. For a spirit does not have flesh and bones as you see that I have" (Luke 24:38-39). Their conviction was based upon solid evidence that could not be disputed.

THE WORD OF LIFE WAS MADE MANIFEST: "The life was made manifest, and we have seen it, and testify to it and proclaim to you the eternal life, which was with the Father and was made manifest to us" (1 John 1:2). The word "manifest" is a Greek word that means to "make openly known." Therefore, John is telling us that it can be openly known that Jesus is the word of life. It is no secret. God the Father made it known to the apostles. By thoroughly investigating the apostles' claims about Jesus, the truth can be clearly seen. The result of believing the truth about Jesus is the reception of eternal life for all who obey Him.

THE LIFE WAS PROCLAIMED AMONG MEN

> That which we have seen and heard we proclaim also to you, so that you too may have fellowship with us; and indeed our fellowship is with the Father and with his Son Jesus Christ. And

we are writing these things so that our joy may be complete.

1 John 1:3-4

The message that the apostles proclaimed not only gave believers an opportunity to obtain eternal life but it also provided them fellowship with the Father, His Son, and the apostles. We can rightly assume that all faithful believers share this same fellowship. We will discuss the topic of fellowship in more detail in Chapter Three.

WRITING TO GIVE COMPLETE JOY: "And we are writing these things so that our joy may be complete" (1 John 1:4). This verse contains the first of five purpose statements that are found in 1 John. The first purpose is to receive complete joy. It is evident from the Bible that joy does not depend upon outward circumstances. Paul wrote to the brethren in the church at Philippi from a prison house. He told them that he prayed for them with joy (Phil. 1:4). He also wrote, "rejoice always; again I will say rejoice" (Phil. 4:4). An encouraging word from faithful brethren is always a source of joy! It brings joy to everyone concerned. That is true for both the writer and the recipients. The epistle of 1 John was written so that our joy may be complete (1 John 1:4).

MORE EVIDENCE THAT CHRIST IS DEITY

The scope of this devotional commentary does not allow for a fuller examination of the Deity of Christ. However, I want to give a few important passages you might want to study for yourselves.

1. **JOHN 1:1-18.** This tremendous passage proclaims that Jesus is the Word, that He was with God, and that he was God. The Word created all things. The Word is Jesus. If you study the passage you will want to notice the key words that are used. The Word (Jesus) became flesh and lived among us. Jesus is the Word. The word is Deity. Jesus is God who became flesh.

2. **COLOSSIANS 1:15-17.** This passage presents Jesus as the image of the

invisible God. Jesus created all things, He is before all things, He is the purpose of creation, and He holds all things together. Jesus is preeminent over all other men. He is God made flesh.

3. PHILIPPIANS 2:6-11. These verses clearly show us that before He was born a man Jesus had equality with God. Yet, He emptied Himself and was born a man. Our Lord humbled himself, and became obedient unto death on a Roman cross. For this reason, God has highly exalted Him. Verses 9-11 tell us that every living being in heaven, on the earth, or under the earth will bow the knee to Jesus and will confess that Jesus Christ is Lord, to the glory of the Father.

4. MATTHEW 16:13. In this verse Jesus asks His apostles the following question. "Who do people say that the Son of Man is?" Compare that to passages that say Christ is the Son of God. Can you see how the phrase "Son of Man" proves Jesus came in the flesh? First John 1:3 calls the Messiah "His Son Jesus Christ". This proves Jesus is the Son of God.

These passages disprove the false teaching being taught by the antichrists in the days of the apostle John. The apostles' testimony in 1 John 1:1-4 proves that Jesus is God and that He came to earth in the flesh.

There are many Old Testament prophecies that relate to Christ's Deity. Study these passages and your faith will be strengthened and you will walk your Christian walk with more confidence. You will also be better equipped to speak with those who deny that Jesus is the Christ, the Son of the living God. Even though we are not eyewitnesses we can still show others the testimony given by the apostle John. We can speak about the Lord Jesus Christ with full assurance that he is all the Bible claimed him to be.

DISCUSSION QUESTIONS:

1. Discuss the statement "They Heard the Lord".
2. Discuss the statement "They saw the Lord".
3. Discuss the statement "They looked upon the Lord".
4. Discuss the statement "They touched Jesus".
5. Discuss the meaning of the phrase "The word of life". Who is the word of life? How was the word of life made manifest?
6. Do you believe Jesus is the Son of God (Meaning that He is Deity)? How would you prove that teaching to others?

CHAPTER THREE

WALKING IN THE LIGHT

1 JOHN 1:5-2:2

> This is the message we have heard from him and proclaim to you, that God is light, and in him is no darkness at all.
>
> 1 John 1:5

In this chapter we will examine the message the apostles heard from God. First John 1:5-10 presents the topics of light, darkness, and the acknowledgement of sin. Chapter 2:1-2 reveals the advocate God gave us to resolve our sin problem. We will see how all of these meaningful concepts are addressed in the space of only eight verses! Isn't that amazing!

You will notice the apostles were given the inspired message that "God is light and in him is no darkness at all." We will take a deeper look at the meaning of light and darkness in the pages to follow. For now just think about the meaning of the statement that God is light. What does that truth about God, our heavenly Father, bring to your mind?

The early Gnostics made a grave mistake when they failed to see the distinction between light and darkness. They did not understand that there is no darkness whatsoever in God! He is light and from Him comes the enlightening news that Jesus is His only begotten Son and the savior of the world. The light found in God is also found in Jesus Christ. This Divine illumination is seen through the light of the Gospel message of salvation. Jesus calls His disciples the light of the world (Matt. 5:14-16). When we let our light shine God is glorified.

SOME THOUGHTS ON LIGHT

LIGHT NEEDS NO WITNESS: Light itself bears witness to its presence. People who are not blind can see when the light is shining. When I served in the US Navy we often went to sea just off the West Coast to conduct war exercises. We often returned to base after the sun had set and darkness was over the face of the water.

I always enjoyed going on deck to see the lights of the California coastline as we sailed back into port. I never went outside in order to see the darkness. The beauty of the moment was seen in the sparkling brightness of the myriad of lights that were spread along the California coastline as far as the eye could see. Spiritually speaking the light of God is being revealed through the gospel. As already mentioned, followers of Jesus are called lights. Light needs no witness. It can be seen by anyone having eyes to see.

In the book of Romans Paul spoke of the Gentiles from the past who refused the light and became "futile in their thinking and their foolish hearts were darkened" (Rom. 1:21). That same darkness will come upon people today if they refuse the light of the Gospel. The Gentiles ended up rejecting God to the point that He gave them up (Rom. 1:24-32). He gave them up because they were spiritually blind and could no longer see the light.

When Jesus came God's light shined more brightly than ever before. Sadly, many of the Jewish religious leaders of the day either would not or could not see the light Jesus revealed to them. Jesus spoke of their inability to see in Matthew

13:13. Can you see the light of God shining when you study your Bible? You can if you have eyes to see. However, "if the blind lead the blind both will fall into a pit" (Matt. 15:14). There is no doubt that light needs no witness. Others can see our light, and when they do, they will glorify the God of heaven.

LIGHT GUIDES: The antichrists (Gnostics) of John's day thought they were the guides who were to lead others to the spiritual light of God. They were not! While people can be lights they are not the source of light. That distinction belongs to Jesus. His godly light shines brightly and reveals God's righteousness to all who seek Him. All of God's children should reflect His light to the lost but we sometimes put our light under a bushel. It is the Christian's responsibility to provide an example for others to follow, "Be imitators of me, as I am of Christ" (1 Cor. 11:1). If the people who know you were to walk just like you walk, where would they spend eternity? Follow Jesus and you will become a guide to others. They will see your light and many will become lights themselves. In this way God is glorified.

I remember the first time I preached in the village of Praw, Thailand. Because of the need for farmers to complete their farm work we did not meet for worship until after dark. The building had no electricity so people brought Coleman lamps with them. My Thai brothers and sisters used their lamps for a dual purpose. They used them to light their path as they came to the building and they also used them to provide light for our worship assembly.

I was fascinated the first time I saw the long string of lights coming towards the building from every direction. It was awesome to see the multitude of lights coming closer and closer to us. I could not but think of Psalm 119:105, "Your word is a lamp to my feet and a light to my path". Jesus said our path towards heaven is narrow and difficult (Matt. 7:13-14). Under such circumstances we truly need God's bright light to guide us on our path. Light has been provided in order to guide us along the narrow pathway. Jesus Himself is light. The word of God, the Bible, is a light that guides us on our way.

LIGHT REVEALS HOLY LIVING: God's light is an impeccable example of holiness. Jesus once quizzed his opponents with the question, "Which one of you convicts me of sin?" John 8:46. Who among us would dare to make such a challenge while standing in the midst of our enemies? If we did so our opponents would dig up some evidence of our past failings and point out our shortcomings for everyone to see. Jesus had no such weaknesses. He was tempted just like the rest of us but He never sinned (Heb. 4:15).

God commands us to "be holy, for I am holy" (1 Pet. 1:16). Peter wrote about the power of Christian living in 1 Peter 4:1-6. First he spoke of the ungodly lifestyle of the Gentiles and then he contrasted that to the lifestyle of believers. Peter summed it up in verse four by saying, "With respect to this they are surprised when you do not join them in the same flood of debauchery, and they malign you." Isn't it sad that so many people not only hate the light but they also malign those who walk in it? Truly the light will reveal holy living to all who have eyes to see.

GOD AND JESUS ARE LIGHT – SO ARE WE: Jesus said, "I am the light of the world. Whoever follows me will not walk in darkness, but will have the light of life" (John 8:12). The light of life refers to the lifestyle of a child of God that leads him to eternal life. Thank God for the light. Remember, "God is light and in him is no darkness at all" (1 John 1:5). It is important to know that we are called to be lights in a dark and sinful world. Being the light is godlike. Shine Christian shine! When we do, it is God who gets the glory!

LIGHT OVERCOMES DARKNESS: "In him was life and the life was the light of men. The light shines in the darkness, and the darkness has not overcome it," (John 1:4-5). Jesus is both the light and the life. When we walk in His light we also become a light to others. When it comes to being victorious light always wins. Enter a dark room and turn on the light and you will experience a graphic illustration of the power of light to overcome darkness.

I know a man who went to prison for crimes he committed. After his release he realized the need to find a better way of life. After a long search he was taught the gospel and became a Christian. After attending a Bible training facility he left

America in order to serve as a missionary. He has served overseas for a number of years. Churches have been planted, preachers have been trained, and souls have been saved through his ministry. His life is a wonderful example of light overcoming darkness! Ever since the day he believed this man has been walking in the light. His life is a powerful testimony to the fact that light destroys darkness.

THOUGHTS ON DARKNESS

DARKNESS REPRESENTS EVIL: If light represents God and all that is good then darkness represents wickedness and the devil's lies. "I know, O Lord, that the way of man is not in himself, that it is not in man who walks to direct his steps" (Jeremiah 10:23). Bright lights chase the darkness out of a room but when the lights go out the darkness prevails. While darkness cannot overcome light it is always possible for someone to turn off the light. We live in a world that is living in spiritual darkness. More and more people do not have the light of God's word. Lets make it our responsibility to live in such a way that we can help others to see the light!

DARKNESS REPRESENTS SEPARATION FROM GOD: Jesus called hell a place of "outer darkness" a place where there will be "weeping and gnashing of teeth" (Matt. 25:30). Religious leaders who are spiritually blind can only lead the souls of men to disaster. "If the blind lead the blind, both will fall into a pit" (Matt. 15:14). They fall into the pit because they cannot see where they are going. Walking in the dark is a sure way to become separated from God.

The beauty of God is that He "is light and in Him is no darkness at all" (1 John 1:5). No individual is compelled to remain separated from God. Jehovah God is "not wishing that any should perish but that all should reach repentance" (2 Pet. 3:9). All who seek Him can find the light and walk in it. Do not allow darkness to separate you from God!

DARKNESS HIDES TRUTH: Light reveals truth while darkness hides it. Those in darkness are either ignorant of God's word or they are deceived. Some teach error as a means of earthly gain. Others teach in order to draw away disciples after themselves. When error is taught and people believe falsehood they are plunged into darkness. "If we say we have fellowship with him while we walk in darkness, we lie and do not practice the truth" (1 John 1:5). Such self-deception is far too common among religious people. We do not have the freedom to serve God in any way that we please. Ours is not the pursuit of personal happiness or monetary gain but ours is the pursuit of God's truth and the salvation of our souls. Darkness hides the truth of God's word.

DARKNESS SEVERS FELLOWSHIP: It is impossible to have fellowship with God while we are walking in darkness (sin). "If we say we have fellowship with him while we walk in darkness, we lie and do not practice the truth" (1 John 1:6). According to John, walking in darkness demonstrates that we are not practicing the truth. Study God's word and you will find the light. By prayerful Bible study "you will know the truth, and the truth will set you free" (John 8:32).

EXPERIENCING FELLOWSHIP

> If we say we have fellowship with him while we walk in darkness, we lie and do not practice the truth. But if we walk in the light, as he is in the light, we have fellowship with one another, and the blood of Jesus his Son cleanses us from all sin.
>
> 1 John 1:6-7

Claiming to have fellowship with God does not guarantee we have it. The scripture above informs us that if we are walking in darkness "we lie and do not practice the truth." Fellowship with God and Christ comes when we practice truth and walk in the light. John gave his apostolic testimony and his words are the truth. Those who desire to have fellowship with God must practice the truth. What is truth? Referring to God we read, "Your word is truth" (John 17:17).

The word "fellowship" comes from the Greek word "koinonia." It means, "the act of partaking, sharing, participation, communion, partners with." Many different English words are used to define the meaning of "koinonia." Context determines which English word should be used when translating the Greek word into English.

Read the following passages to gain a better understanding of its meaning. When a passage uses an English word other than fellowship it will be underlined.

1. Fellowship is something we expect to have with each other and with Deity. "That which we have seen and heard we proclaim also to you, so that you too may have fellowship with us; and indeed our fellowship is with the Father and with his Son Jesus Christ" (1 John 1:3).
2. Fellowship with God is found when we do not walk in darkness. "If we say we have fellowship with him while we walk in darkness, we lie and do not practice the truth" (1 John 1:6).
3. Fellowship with Jesus is provided by God. "God is faithful, by whom you were called into the fellowship of his Son, Jesus Christ our Lord" (1 Cor. 1:9).
4. Fellowship describes our relationship with the Holy Spirit. "If there is any encouragement in Christ, any comfort from love, any participation (fellowship) in the Spirit, 2complete my joy by being of the same mind" (Phil. 2:1-2).
5. Fellowship describes how we share in the suffering of Jesus. "That I may know him and the power of his resurrection, and may share (fellowship) his sufferings, becoming like him in his death" (Phil. 3:10).
6. Fellowship describes the unity that existed between the apostles and the believers who accepted their teaching. "And they devoted themselves to the apostles' teaching and fellowship" (Acts 2:42).
7. Fellowship describes the relationship between faithful brethren. "They gave the right hand of fellowship to Barnabas and me" (Gal. 2:9).
8. Fellowship describes the sharing of financial needs with those who

preach the word. "No church entered into partnership [fellowship] with me in giving and receiving, except you only" (Phil. 4:15).

9. Fellowship describes our Christian walk. "If we walk in the light as he is in the light we have fellowship with one another, and the blood of Jesus his Son cleanses us from all sin" (1 John 1:7).

It is important to understand that it is possible to have fellowship with our fellow man and still have *no fellowship* with God. When we get it right we will experience fellowship with God and with each other. See the chart below for a simplistic look at fellowship. The two arrows represent two people who have fellowship with God. The dotted line represents the fellowship two believers share with each other because of the fellowship they have with God and with Jesus.

FELLOWSHIP WITH GOD & JESUS

PRODUCES FELLOWSHIP WITH EACH OTHER

WALKING IN THE LIGHT

> If we walk in the light as he is in the light, we have fellowship with one another, and the blood of Jesus his Son cleanses us from all sin.
>
> 1 John 1:7

To walk in the light indicates action and direction. Being a child of God is a lifestyle. We are not to sit around like spectators who are waiting for Jesus to come again. We do not sit calmly in a worship assembly waiting for God to bless our lives. The Christian experience is one of movement. We are *walking* in the light—not *sitting* in it! We have *direction* and we are on the move. We are walking in the steps of Jesus. Such a walk produces the kind of life that leads to eternal life. Read Matthew 16:24-27 to consider some detailed attributes of the disciple who denies himself and follows Jesus. When the light that illuminates our life is the light of Jesus then we have fellowship with Him.

Fellowship requires that we have a proper relationship with God and with other believers. Everyone who is walking in the light has been cleansed from all of his sins by the blood of Jesus Christ. Far too many people claim to follow Jesus but do not have the proper walk. To be pleasing to God we must be *walking*. We must also travel in the right *direction*. It is only when we walk where Jesus walked that His blood will cleanse us from all of our sin. Then we are truly walking in the light as He is in the light.

ACKNOWLEDGING OUR SIN

> If we say we have no sin, we deceive ourselves, and the truth is not in us. If we confess our sins, he is faithful and just to forgive us our sins and to cleanse us from all unrighteousness. If we say we have not sinned, we make him a liar and his word is not in us.
>
> 1 John 1:8-10

Walking in the light does not mean that we never sin. The antichrists denied the presence of individual sin in their own lives. They believed if a person knew enough he would be able to overcome sin by his knowledge. They believed that knowledge could remove any possibility of sin in their lives. John destroys this argument in 1 John 1:8-10. He does so by presenting the futility of denying our present sins. He also presents the need for us to confess our sins. He also teaches us to acknowledge our past sins.

DENIAL OF PRESENT SINS: "If we say we have no sin, we deceive ourselves, and the truth is not in us" (1 John 1:8). In the Greek language this sentence is written in the present active indicative. This tense indicates *continual action*. The truth is, even after we become children of God we continue to struggle with sin. According to 1 John 1:8, a Christian cannot claim he no longer sins. John makes it clear that anyone making such a claim is deceiving himself and the truth is not in him. Do not lie to yourself in regard to your sin problem by claiming you no longer sin. We must be constantly on our guard against the many temptations we face in life. Do not fall for the devil's lie that once a person becomes a child of God he cannot sin.

CONFESS OUR SINS: "If we confess our sins, he is faithful and just to forgive us our sins and to cleanse us from all unrighteousness" (1 John 1:9). John is speaking to believers in this passage. To confess means, "To speak, or say the same together with another; to assent, accord, agree with, hence, to concede, admit, confess." Why is it that so many people who name the name of Jesus refuse to admit their faults either to man or to God? Sometimes we don't even acknowledge our sins to ourselves. It could be because of pride or shame. With others it is simply ignorance about the need to examine their own personal conduct. When we do sin we must acknowledge our shortcomings before God.

When a believer is baptized into Christ all of his sins are washed away (Acts 22:16). His baptism (immersion) is into the death, burial, and resurrection of Christ (Rom. 6:1-7). However, we need to understand that it is possible for a person to sin after he becomes a Christian. When that happens we need additional forgiveness and cleansing.

We do not need to be baptized again but we do need to repent and confess our wrongdoing. The word repentance is from the Greek word "metanoia" meaning "a change of will produced by sorrow for sins, leading to reformation of life." When we do this, the Lord will cleanse us from all unrighteousness and restore our status as a faithful child of God.

Unfortunately, acknowledgement of sin apart from repentance is worthless. When we sin we must confess our wrongdoing. In some circumstances, it is necessary to acknowledge our sin to the person(s) we wronged (Matt. 5:23-24; 18:15-18). When we confess our sins and repent we are restored to faithfulness.

Read Acts 8:9-24 to learn about a man named Simon. This man was very highly regarded by the citizens of Samaria. He appeared to have special miraculous powers. Therefore the people called him "Great." He was not really a miracle worker. He was a trickster. When Simon heard the gospel message he obeyed God's commandments and became a Christian. However, when the apostles Peter and John came for a visit they laid hands on some of the new believers. These people received a miraculous gift by the power of the Holy Spirit.

Simon wanted to buy "the gift of God with money" (Acts 8:20). He wanted the power to lay hands on people in order to give them a miraculous gift. Because his motive was sinful, Peter rebuked him as a wicked man who was in the bond of iniquity. Remember Simon was a new Christian. However, he was already in need of confession and repentance. To his credit, he asked Peter to pray for him so that he would be delivered from the consequences of his sin.

It is amazing to learn that even an apostle can sin. In Galatians 2:11-14 the apostle Paul opposed Peter to his face because he stood condemned. Read the text to learn that Peter became a hypocrite by drawing back from the Gentile Christians when certain Jewish believers arrived in town. The mistake of Peter was so great that even Barnabas followed his example and committed the same sin. Paul stated that the actions of Peter were "not in step with the truth of the gospel". The actions of both Peter and Barnabas were wrong. Paul rebuked them for their error in order to bring them back to the light. One must never ignore his personal sin. Doing so creates a real danger to his eternal destiny. Even worse, our sins sometimes cause others to sin right along with us. When we do sin we must repent and confess our sins. Our faithful Father will forgive us and we will again be considered to be faithful children.

DENIAL OF PAST SINS: "If we say we have not sinned, we make him a liar and his word is not in us" (1 John 1:10). This is different from 1:8, which speaks of those who were denying present sins. The structure of verse 10 in the Greek indicates a denial that they ever sinned in the past. It seems that some people looked back on their lives and erroneously concluded they had never sinned. This belief is totally false. Jesus Christ is the only human being who ever lived a sinless life. Scripture clearly states that "all have sinned and fall short of the glory of God" (Rom.3:23). The apostle John teaches us that if we claim to be sinless we make God a liar! Hebrews 6:18 informs us that it is impossible for God to lie.

It is important for every believer to acknowledge that he was a sinner in the past. A failure to do so makes God a liar. Therefore, we learn from this passage that we must acknowledge two kinds of sin in our lives: (1) Our present sins and (2) our past sins. We must also confess our sins before God, the Father.

THE SOLUTION TO THE SIN PROBLEM

> My little children, I am writing these things to you so that you may not sin. But if anyone does sin, we have an advocate with the Father, Jesus Christ the righteous. He is the propitiation for our sins, and not for ours only but also for the sins of the whole world.
>
> 1 John 2:1-2

We are now ready to discuss the solution to the sin problem. This is an important topic. When John addressed the believers as little children he was not speaking to them in a demeaning way. Perhaps he used this language because of his advanced age. Some believe John used this type of language because the recipients were new Christians. A similar usage is found in the following passage, "Like newborn infants, long for the pure spiritual milk, that by it you may grow up to salvation" (1 Pet. 2:2).

As children, we are all in the same family. Our nationality or the color of our skin does not matter. It makes no difference whether we are male or female. We are family. "There is neither Jew nor Greek, there is neither slave nor free, there is neither male nor female, for you are all one in Christ Jesus. And if you are Christ's, then you are Abraham's offspring, heirs according to promise" (Gal. 3:28-29). It is heart warming to know that all believers are childern of God.

In Chapter Two of this commentary we learned five purpose statements John gave for writing 1 John. Here is the second one. "I am writing these things to you so that you may not sin" (1 John 2:1). God would be well pleased if converts lived their entire lives without commiting a single sin. John encourages us to do just that. However, sometimes, even when we give it our best effort, we fall short of our goal and we sin. What provision has God made for us to give us the victory over our sin problem? Below is John's solution.

JESUS OUR ADVOCATE: "If anyone does sin, we have an advocate with the Father, Jesus Christ the righteous" (1 John 2:1). An advocate is "one called to the aid of another. An intercessor, advocate." Jesus knows our frailties. He came to earth as a man and suffered the same physical ailments and temptations everyone else experiences. Yes, He was tempted in all ways, just like we are, but without sin (Heb. 4:15). Jesus is qualified to stand in the gap between us and God. He is our advocate. In this way, God shows us how Jesus helps us with our sin problem. He intercedes on our behalf.

JESUS OUR RIGHTEOUSNESS: Jesus Himself is righteous. When we have faith in Him Jesus becomes our righteousness (1 Cor. 1:30). In regard to Jesus, righteous means, "fulfilling all claims which are right and becoming; just as it should be; a right state, of which God is the standard." The righteousness of every faithful person from Adam onward had his righteousness imputed to them because of their faith. Faithful "Abraham believed God and it was counted [imputed] to him as righteousness" (Rom. 4:3). We don't deserve our righteous status but we receive it anyway. Why? Because of our faith. Since it is imputed to us we have no room for boasting. We certainly don't deserve such a gift. It is awesome that a sinful man could be called righteous. It is only possible because Jesus is our righteousness. In this way, through His righteousness, God provides a solution to our sin problem.

JESUS OUR PROPITIATION: The word, "propitiation," means "concilliation, expiation." It is described by some teachers as a covering. In this sense, when we repent of our sins God sees only the blood of Jesus. It is His precious blood, His sacrifice, that provides the means for our forgiveness. Only Jesus' blood is able to remove sin. Therefore, whether we are a sinner looking for forgiveness or a child of God struggling against sin, Jesus provides the propitiation for our sins. He not only pleads our case, He pays the required price for our forgiveness. He is the concilliation (propitiation) for our sins. Only Jesus can bring us back into a friendly relationship with God. What a wonderful Savior we have! Jesus provides the solution to our sin problem. He is our *advocate*, our *righteous* and the *propitiation* for our sins. Thank God, our sin problem is solved through Jesus Christ our Lord!

DISCUSSION QUESTIONS:

1. What does statement "God is light" bring to your mind?
2. What does it mean to you to walk in the light as Jesus walked in the light?
3. Write the points under "Thoughts on Light"? Discuss them.
4. What were the four points under "Thoughts on Darkness"? Discuss them.
5. Discuss the different ways fellowship is used in the Bible.
6. Discuss the meaning of 1 John 1:8.
7. How important is 1 John 1:9?
8. Discuss the meaning of 1 John 1:10.
9. Discuss these important words found in 1 John 2:1-2
    - ADVOCATE
    - RIGHTEOUSNESS
    - PROPITIATION

CHAPTER FOUR

SEPARATION FROM THE WORLD

1 JOHN 2:3-17

> And by this we know that we have come to know him, if we keep his commandments. Whoever says "I know him" but does not keep his commandments is a liar, and the truth is not in him, but whoever keeps his word, in him truly the love of God is perfected. By this we may know that we are in him: whoever says he abides in him ought to walk in the same way in which he walked.
>
> 1 John 2:3-6

In this chapter we will examine how to prove that we know God. Many people claim to know the Lord but, in fact, they really don't know Him at all. What is it that proves that we know God? We prove it by keeping his commandments. Failure to obey makes us liars. It also shows that the truth is not in us.

Do you find it surprising that keeping God's commandments perfects the love of God? The kind of love God wants us to have flows two ways. It flows from God to us and from us to God. His love is not perfected unless His people keep His commandments. We will also notice that those who claim to abide in him must walk the same way He (God) walks. Go back to 1 John 1:7 to be reminded that we are to walk in the light as He (Jesus) is in the light. When we are doing the will of God we are walking in the midst of both the Father and the Son. How comforting is that?

Have you ever considered keeping the commandments as proof that you loved God? If not, you better reconsider! It is easy to say, "I love Him" but it becomes meaningless words if you do not keep His commandments. For example, the Pharisees of Jesus' day spoke the right message but they did not obey God's commandments. Jesus said, "The scribes and the Pharisees sit on Moses' seat, so do and observe whatever they tell you, but not the works they do. For they preach, but do not practice" (Matt.23:2-3). How sad to learn that the religious rulers of Jesus' day preached the right message but failed to practice what they preached. Consequently Jesus called them hypocrites (Matt. 23:13). The proof that we love God is found when our walk matches our talk. Our love for God is not measured by words alone. It is measured by the combination of what we say and what we do. James put it this way, "But be doers of the word, and not hearers only, deceiving yourselves" (Jas. 1:22).

BROTHERLY LOVE

> Beloved, I am writing you no new commandment, but an old commandment that you had from the beginning. The old commandment is the word that you have heard. At the same time, it is a new commandment that I am writing to you, which is true in him and in you, because the darkness is passing away and the true light is already shining.
>
> 1 John 2:7-8

This section begins by calling the brethren "beloved." The word means "the deliberate exercise of the judgment; the giving of a decided preference to one person out of many." It is not a phrase we often hear in modern day Christianity. This term is usually reserved for expressions of love between a husband and wife. Or, sometimes it is used as a term of endearment between parent and child. When was the last time someone called you "beloved"? Or better yet, when was the last time you called a fellow Christian "beloved"? Try it and notice the reaction of the one to whom you speak. Are they shocked? Befuddled? Do we really count our brothers and sisters in Christ so dearly that we consider them to be our beloved? If not—why not?

John now compares an old commandment to the new one. Both deal with the topic of love. Jesus referred to the old commandment when a lawyer of the Pharisees asked Him, "Teacher, which is the greatest commandment in the Law?" Read Matthew 22:34-40. The lawyers and rabbis argued over this question often and they could not come to a satisfactory answer. They hoped to make Jesus look bad by asking Him a question that He could not answer. However, Jesus was able to answer the question without any hesitation. In fact, the Lord listed the two greatest commandments. The greatest is to love God with all our being and the second is to love our neighbor as ourselves. In His response, Jesus cited Deuteronomy 6:5 and Leviticus 19:18 respectively. To love God and to love your neighbor as yourselves are the greatest commandments. That is the old commandment referred to in 1 John 2:7.

However, there is a new commandment for Christians. Jesus gave this new commandment in John 13:34-35. "A new commandment I give to you, that you love one another: just as I have loved you, you also are to love one another. By this all people will know that you are my disciples, if you have love for one another." What is "new" about Jesus' commandment? Loving one another is not new. We have already read how Jesus spoke of brotherly love from the Old Testament law.

Jesus commanded us to love each other "just as I have loved you." How much did Jesus love us? He loved us enough to give His life for us. That is what is new. How dedicated are you to keeping that commandment? It requires total commitment.

MORE ABOUT LIGHT AND DARKNESS

> Whoever says he is in the light and hates his brother is still in darkness. Whoever loves his brother abides in the light, and in him there is no cause for stumbling. But whoever hates his brother is in the darkness and walks in the darkness, and does not know where he is going, because the darkness has blinded his eyes.
>
> 1 John 2:9-11

Anyone who claims to walk in the light but hates his brother is still in darkness. It is by loving our brother that we prove we abide in the light. Abide means "to remain, abide, dwell." One of my instructors once told me to abide means to settle down and make a permanent dwelling place. Such a person will not stumble.

If you hate your brother you are still in darkness. That is true in spite of any claim you make to be walking in the light. John goes so far as to say that such a person is "in the darkness and walks in the darkness, and does not know where he is going, because the darkness has blinded his eyes" (1 John 2:11). There is nothing sadder than seeing brothers and sisters in Christ hating each other. Such people cannot see clearly because they are in darkness. Such a one "does not know where he is going, because the darkness has blinded his eyes" (1 John 2:11). Hate is the cause for "stumbling" in the dark.

It should grieve us to see family members having enmity against each other. We have all seen families who are estranged from each other to the point that they refuse to have anything to do with their family members. This is certainly not how God would have us live. What is true for physical families is doubly true in the church of our Lord Jesus Christ. We must not – we cannot hate our brothers and sisters in Christ. We are to love them as Christ loved us. Failure to love one another as Christ loved us proves one is spiritually blind.

One might ask the question "What, then, are we to do when hatred exists between brethren?" Or, "What are we to do if a brother refuses to be reconciled with us?" Jesus provides the answer.

SETTLE ISSUES QUICKLY: Do not allow problems to fester and grow even larger. Jesus said, "If you are offering your gift at the altar and there remember that you brother has something against you, leave your gift there before the altar and go. First be reconciled to your brother and then come and offer your gift" (Matt. 5:23-24). The longer you wait the more difficult it is going to be to get things right. Nip your problems in the bud while they are more manageable. The longer you wait the bigger the problem becomes. Don't wait until the issue is so big that love has turned into hatred.

ADMIT YOUR OWN GUILT: Whenever problems arise between brethren it is usually a two way street. That is, both parties had a part in creating the problem. Be humble and admit your part in causing the discord. The simple words "I'm sorry!" can go a long way towards solving issues. Don't let the devil get a stronghold on your attitude. When David was made aware of his sin with Bathsheba he did not hesitate to admit his guilt before the prophet Nathan and before God. David told the prophet, "I have sinned against the Lord" (2 Sam. 12:13). Be humble and try to restore broken relationships with your brothers and sisters in Christ quickly.

GET HELP: If you can't settle the problem yourself find a mediator to assist you in restoring harmony between you and the offended brother. Jesus gave us guidelines on how to restore fellowship and love between brothers with problems in Matt. 18:15-17. Read the Biblical text and then read the steps listed below.

1. The first thing that should be done is to try to settle the issue one-on-one. Just the two of you. Address the problem in a way that fellowship can be restored. If both parties agree to forgive or solve the problem then everything is settled. Be sure to express your love one for another when fellowship has been restored!
2. If the person won't listen to you, find one or two witnesses and make another effort to solve the issue that exists between you and your brother.

If this meeting is successful, you will have restored the relationship with your brother. If not, there is one more step that must be taken.

3. If your brother still won't reconcile with you take the issue to the church. If this final step doesn't bring a solution to the problem the offender should be considered as a Gentile (one outside of Christ) or a tax collector. The Jews of Jesus' day considered tax collectors to be sinners (Matt. 9:9-13). Therefore when they spoke of them they lumped them in with other people whom they considered to be sinners. While tax collectors probably were sinners it was the self-righteous Jewish leaders of the day who judged them as such.

The requirement to love our brothers and sisters in Christ is an imperative. If we are to please God we have no choice. In 1 John 4:20 we learn that anyone who claims to love God while hating his brother is a liar. That is strong language! Do your best to love your brethren in Christ, your family members, and the lost. This is not easy. It can be a difficult task! However, God will bless you when you do. And – you will be walking in the light along with Jesus and God.

A person that hates his brother "is in the darkness and walks in the darkness, and does not know where he is going, because the darkness has blinded his eyes," 1 John 2:11. This teaching is simple to understand. Loving your brother is evidence you are walking in light. Hating your brother is evidence you are blind and walking in darkness. It is easy to understand but is very difficult to accomplish. Pray that God will help you to love those people you know that are difficult to love. After all, God does love *you*! I don't know about you but I stand in awe of the awesome God who loves "unlovable" me. When it comes to loving my brothers how can I do any less?

ABIDING IN GOD'S WORD

I am writing to you, little children, because your sins are forgiv-

> en for his name's sake. I am writing to you, fathers, because you know him who is from the beginning. I am writing to you, young men, because you have overcome the evil one. I write to you, children, because you know the Father. I write to you, fathers, because you know him who is from the beginning. I write to you, young men, because you are strong, and the word of God abides in you, and you have overcome the evil one.
>
> 1 John 2:12-14

John now addresses believers who are at three different levels of maturity. He speaks to people that are children, fathers, and young men. He speaks to each group twice. It is likely that John is not speaking of their physical age but their levels of spiritual maturity.

CHILDREN: (Those who are immature.) "Your sins are forgiven for his name's sake (1 John 2:12). This is true because they have obeyed the gospel. It is also said of the children that they "know the Father" (1 John 2:13). One cannot become a child of God unless he knows God. This helps us understand that we must be taught in order to become a child of God. "For they shall all know me, from the least of them to the greatest" (Heb. 8:11).

FATHERS: (Those who are the most mature.) "You know him who is from the beginning," (1 John 2:13a, 14a). Mature Christians "believe that God exists and that he rewards those who seek him" (Heb. 11:6). Faith is one of the three great attributes mentioned in 1 Cor. 13:13. Faith is something that continues to grow with maturity. The mature are certain about who God is and about the reward He will give to the faithful.

YOUNG MEN: (Those in the process of becoming more mature.) The young men have overcome the evil one (1 John 2:13). A faithful child of God will never forget the day he was immersed in water and his sins were washed away (Acts 22:16). The day they obeyed the gospel was the day they overcame the devil. We must never forget that meaningful day. In verse 14 we learn that young men in the Lord "are strong, and the word of God abides in you." By knowledge of Scripture and the faith it provides the young men can "resist the devil and he will flee from you" (Jas. 4:7).

All believers belong in one of the categories listed in 1 John 2:12-14. Everyone, regardless of their level of maturity must grow in their faith so that they can remain faithful to the Lord.

DO NOT LOVE THE WORLD!

> Do not love the world or the things in the world. If anyone loves the world, the love of the Father is not in him. For all that is in the world—the desires of the flesh and the desires of the eyes and pride of life—is not from the Father but is from the world. And the world is passing away along with its desires, but whoever does the will of God abides forever.
>
> 1 John 2:15-17

We just discussed the new commandment that Jesus gave to us. We learned we are to love one other as Jesus loves us. Now we will study a forbidden kind of love. We are commanded not to love the world. What does that mean? Here are some ways the word "world" is used in the Bible.

THE PHYSICAL WORLD: According to Genesis 1:31, the physical world is very good. Therefore, this is not the world the Apostle is referencing. We can certainly love a beautiful sunset, a majestic mountain, or the beautiful flowers that grow in the meadow. We are not forbidden to love God's creation.

HUMANS: Mankind is called the world in John 3:16. You know the passage. "For God so loved the world that he gave his only Son, that whoever believes in him should not perish but have eternal life" (John 3:16). There is no way that 1

John 2:15-17 refers to mankind when he commanded us not to love the world. We must not hate what God loves. It is not mankind that we are to hate.

THE SINFUL WORLD: Now we are getting to the meaning of this passage. The sinful things of the world are exactly the things we are forbidden to love. Sinful man has the ability to pervert what is good and make it evil. When men fall to the temptations of the devil they corrupt the good world God created. It is sad to see the state of the world in the 21st century. Sin is running rampant throughout our country and the world. That is because mankind loves sinful activities more than they love God who created this world. When we love the world, the love of the Father is not in us.

The word of God describes the characteristics of the sinful world as "the desires of the flesh and the desires of the eyes and pride of life" (1 John 2:16). We must not love the sinful things found in the world. This passage gives us three categories of things we must not love.

DESIRES OF THE FLESH: A list of fleshly desires is found in Galatians 5:19-21 and 1 Corinthians 6:9-11. These passages well describe the type of sins children of God must shun. Many other verses of scripture identify sins of the flesh we should avoid.

What are we to do to avoid the desires of the flesh? It is important that we learn how to turn off the television set when it displays movies that cater to carnal fleshly desires. The Internet provides pornography for anyone desiring to view it. Jesus said, "I say to you that everyone who looks at a woman with lustful intent has already committed adultery with her in his heart" (Matt. 5:28). We must abstain from sexual activities except with our mates. We must exercise self-control over our fleshly desires. If we don't we will lose our soul.

Romans 1:19-31 speaks of the Gentile world that had grown so sinful that God gave them up and as a result they lost their heavenly reward. "For this reason God gave them up to dishonorable passions" (Rom. 1:26). It is not only sexual sins that fall under the desires of the flesh. It would also include rejecting the existence of

God and worshipping ourselves as if we were God. It could be to lust after material possessions or the pleasures of life. After all, Paul said we should put to death "covetousness which is idolatry" (Col. 3:5). Do not allow fleshly desires to control your life.

DESIRES OF THE EYES: Job wrote, "I have made a covenant with my eyes: how then could I gaze at a virgin?" (Job 31:1). This speaks of the sins brought about by what we see. This would include anything we look at that would cause us to have an inordinate desire for that object. It is much more than unauthorized sexual activities. When the devil tempted Eve she fell for his lies. Only then did she look upon the tree of the knowledge of good and evil with eyes that "saw the tree was good for food and that it was a delight to the eyes, and that the tree was to be desired to make one wise". It was then that "she took of its fruit and ate" (Gen. 3:6). Don't be deceived; the desires of your eyes can lead you into sin.

PRIDE OF LIFE: This includes the love of money, arrogance, ambition, ancestry, past accomplishments, or any of a host of things that become evil, not because they are inherently evil but because of our pride in possessing them. These things become sinful when they become the goal of our life. The sin of pride is likely the forerunner of the list of things that can become sinful under the banner *pride in possessions*. Read James 4:6-10 to receive ample warning against sinful pride. "God opposes the proud but gives grace to the humble."

In 1 John 2:17 we are reminded that, "This world is passing away along with its desires." At best, our desire for worldly things will only last during our lifetime. When we die—then what? Yes the world will pass away but those who obey God's commandments will abide in heaven forever. We would be wise to remind ourselves that "our citizenship is in heaven" (Phil. 3:20). Jesus has prepared a room for us (John 14:1-6). Those who are afflicted by inordinate desires of the flesh, desires of the eyes, or the pride of life cannot receive the crown of life.

The passage concludes with these words. "The world is passing away along with its desires, but whoever does the will of God abides forever" (1 John 2:17).

Getting to heaven is a matter of the will. The devil pits the will of God against human will. When we do God's will the devil is defeated and we will receive our reward. We must maintain separation from the world.

JOHN'S SEVENFOLD TEST

We conclude this chapter by looking at a seven-fold test based on 1 John 1-2.

1. Are you walking in the light (1:7)?
2. Do you admit that, even now, you sometimes sin (1:8-10)?
3. Are you keeping God's commandments (2:4)?
4. Do you abide in Him and walk like Christ (2:6)?
5. Do you love your brothers (2:10)?
6. Do you hate the sinful world (2:15-17)?
7. Do you practice righteousness (2:29)? In the next chapter, when we study 1 John 2:29, we will discuss righteousness in more detail.

We must test ourselves in order to measure the progress we are making in our walk with God. By God's grace we can pass the test but, to do so, we must examine ourselves daily lest we also be disqualified (1 Corinthians 9:27).

DISCUSSION QUESTIONS:

1. According to John, what is the proof that you know God?
2. Name two consequences for the person that does not keep God's commandments (1 John 2:4).
3. Discuss the difference between the "old commandment" and the "new" one.
4. Who is John speaking to when he mentions "children, Fathers, and young

men"?

5. List the ways the word "world" is used in scripture.
6. Discuss the desires of the flesh, the desires of the eyes, and the pride of life.
7. List and discuss John's sevenfold test showing that we walk in the light. Pick one of these points where you have a weakness and make it your goal to strengthen that weakness. (Did you take the sevenfold test? If so, how did you do?)

CHAPTER FIVE

ABIDING IN HIM

1 JOHN 2:18-29

WARNING ABOUT ANTICHRISTS

> Children, it is the last hour, and as you have heard that antichrist is coming, so now many antichrists have come. Therefore we know that it is the last hour. They went out from us, but they were not of us; for if they had been of us, they would have continued with us. But they went out, that it might become plain that they all are not of us.
>
> 1 John 2:18-19

In the first part of this passage we are introduced to a group of Christian teachers from the first century called antichrists. Yes it is true! There were already many men identified as antichrists when John wrote 1 John. The text tells us there were many of them. The term means "against Christ." These men were teaching religious error. It is important to understand that they were part of the congregation to whom John wrote. They were teaching that Jesus did not come in the flesh. They also denied that He was the Son of God.

The passage begins by informing the brethren that the antichrists were predicted in the past and were now among them. He calls it the last hour meaning the prediction of their coming was currently being fulfilled. It is not a declaration of the end of time. The antichrists went out from the apostles (were once faithful men) but were no longer of them (were now teaching error). These statements are meant to make it plain to the brethren that the antichrists were not of "us". That is, they were no longer faithful teachers. When we study 1 John 4:1-6 we will study the sad truth that there have always been false prophets among God's people. The antichrists were part of that number.

These teachers were presenting an early form of what came to be known as Gnosticism. Their doctrine is false and cannot be supported by the word of God. Later in his Epistles John will identify the antichrists (plural) as deceivers. The antichrists were already in the churches teaching false doctrines about the Deity of Christ. The apostle will completely destroy their errors in the books of First and Second John. Simply put, anyone who teaches that Jesus did not come in the flesh or that He is not the Son of God is antichrist. The lesson to be learned from 1 John 2:18-19 is: *the antichrists are not of us.*

WHEN WILL ANTICHRIST COME?

Because so many religious groups believe in the appearance of a single person called the Antichrist at the end of time it is necessary that we address this teaching. The premise is: after His second coming Jesus will reign on earth, in Jerusalem, for 1,000 years. During this time the Lord Jesus will fight against the Antichrist and ultimately prevail. Those who support this theory go to the book of Revelation chapter twenty in order to support their theory that Jesus will reign upon this earth for 1,000 years.

However, take a close look at the passage in Revelation 20 and you will see there is absolutely no mention of antichrist. As a matter of fact, there is no mention of the Antichrist anywhere in the book of Revelation. Antichrists, plural, are only mentioned in the Epistles of John and he says they were already at work among the brethren during his lifetime. Unlike the theoretical Antichrist predicted by many, the ones John mentioned did not have miraculous powers. They were common ordinary men who were teaching falsehood.

People who believe in the coming of a powerful adversary called the Antichrist say he will appear at the end of time. However, 2 Peter 3:10-13 presents an entirely different picture of what will happen when Jesus returns. Peter tells us the heavens will be set on fire and dissolved. In addition, the heavenly bodies will melt as they burn. Read 1 Thessalonians 4:13-18 to learn what will happen when Jesus returns. First of all, the dead saints will rise from the dead and be changed. Then they will meet the Lord in the air – not on this earth. After the dead are raised those who are alive when Jesus returns will also be changed. They will also go to meet the Lord in the air. Paul then tells us that once we meet Him in the air "we will always be with the Lord" (1 Thess. 4:17). Where will we meet Jesus? In the air! How long will we be with Him? Always! There is no mention of Jesus reigning in Jerusalem or anywhere else on earth for a period of 1,000 years. According to Peter the world will be destroyed!

JESUS OUR HIGH PRIEST

The book of Hebrews helps us understand the High Priesthood of Jesus. Read on to see that Jesus, our High Priest, cannot come back to this earth to reign as a Priest. Yet, He *is* now reigning.

JESUS IS NOW OUR HIGH PRIEST. "Jesus has gone as a forerunner on our behalf having become a high priest forever after the order of Melchizedek" (Heb. 6:20). Study all of Hebrews chapter seven to learn that our Lord is now a High Priest after the order of Melchizedek. He will serve as priest forever. Then read Hebrews 9:11-28 to learn that Jesus ascended into heaven, not an earthly temple, in order to offer His blood on our behalf. The Lord did not enter the Holy Place located in Jerusalem but the one located in heaven. Don't lose sight of the fact that Jesus is already serving as our High Priest. Scripture says that He will serve as High Priest forever.

A CHANGE IN THE PRIESTHOOD REQUIRED A CHANGE IN THE LAW. "For when there is a change in the priesthood, there is necessarily a change in the law as well" (Heb. 7:12). Jesus' appointment as High Priest required that the law be changed. When did this change in the law take place? It happened when the Old Law was nailed to the cross (Col. 2:14-15).

Let me explain. The first law God gave to mankind was called the law of sin and death. It was given by God to Adam and Eve (Gen. 2:16-17). All mankind was under that law. This law says that when a person sins he dies spiritually. This law was in effect from Adam to the cross. Romans 8:2 informs us that "the law of the Spirit of life has set you free in Christ Jesus from the law of sin and death". On the cross Jesus Christ set us free from the law of sin and death.

The Law of Moses was received on Mount Sinai and was given to the children of Israel. It was never given to the Gentile world. Therefore the Gentiles remained under the law of sin and death until the cross. Patriarchs were given God's law through the prophets by dreams and visions. Israel, however, was greatly benefited by receiving the Law God gave through Moses. It also lasted until the cross. Both laws were nailed to the cross of Jesus. After His death Jesus mediated a new law for both Jews and for Gentiles (Heb. 9:15-16). This law is in effect beginning with the Christian age and lasting forever. The new law was first proclaimed on the day of Pentecost when 3,000 souls were baptized into Christ (Acts 2:1-47). A change in the priesthood demanded a change in the Law. The new law is contained in the Gospel of Christ and is recorded in the writings of the New Testament.

JESUS CANNOT BE A HIGH PRIEST ON EARTH: "Now if he (speaking of Jesus) were on earth, he would not be a priest at all, since there are priests who offer gifts according to the law" (Heb. 8:4). The psalmist prophesied that Jesus would be "a priest forever after the order of Melchizedek" (Psa.110:4). Jesus became High Priest when he ascended into heaven. He will remain High Priest forever. If Hebrews 8:4 is true, and it is, then any theory that Jesus will literally return to this earth to reign for 1,000 years is false. That is because there are already men serving as priests upon this earth. For this reason, Jesus cannot be a priest on this physical earth. The Bible says Jesus will serve as High Priest forever and ever.

OUR ANOINTING

> But you have been anointed by the Holy One, and you all have knowledge. I write to you, not because you do not know the truth, but because you know it, and because no lie is of the truth. Who is the liar but he who denies that Jesus is the Christ? This is the antichrist, he who denies the Father and the Son. No one who denies the Son has the Father. Whoever confesses the Son has the Father also.
>
> 1 John 2:20-23

The Greek word anointing is "chrisma." In Bullinger's Lexicon of New Testament Words, he defines the anointing as follows. "The anointing, which was emblematic of the Spirit descending and abiding upon." Some see the use of the word anointing as a play on words that compares the antichrists to the Christians. The word Christ "anointed". The antichrists were against the Anointed One, Christ, while the Christians were for Him. The Holy One is the one who anointed the believers.

This anointing comes from the Holy One. It is logical to believe the Holy One mentioned in this passage is the Holy Spirit. Children of God are indwelled (anointed) by the Holy Spirit. It is through the Holy Spirit that human authors wrote the Holy Scriptures. Through Him we receive knowledge and are able to understand the difference between the truth and the lies of the antichrists. This passage provides much needed encouragement for the child of God when he is faced with false teachings. In verse 21 John gives his third purpose statement, "I write to you, not because you do not know the truth, but because you know it." Simply put, John said he wrote because you know the truth.

John now asks a question. "Who is the liar but he who denies that Jesus is the Christ?" The answer is clear. It is the antichrists. They were denying Christ and God, the Father. If you know the truth you know that God is the Father and Jesus is His Son. This passage demonstrates two errors being made by the antichrists: (1) They denied Jesus was God's Anointed (Christ) and (2) This resulted in a denial of both the Father and the Son.

John reminds his readers that their knowledge helped them to know that no lie was of the truth. Do not fall for the lies of the antichrists. True believers confess the Father and the Son.

ABIDE IN THE TEACHING

> Let what you heard from the beginning abide in you. If what you heard from the beginning abides in you, then you too will abide in the Son and in the Father. And this is the promise that he made to us—eternal life.
>
> 1 John 2:24-25

Look back to the day you became a believer in Jesus. Remember what you learned about Him that day. You confessed that He was the Christ, the Son of the living God. You obeyed the Gospel. The truth you learned in the beginning of your walk with God will equip you to remain steadfast when someone lies to you about Jesus.

As we just noted in 1 John 2:20-23 the antichrists were liars because they denied Jesus was the Christ. By doing so they were also denying the Father. Jesus once said, "Everyone who acknowledges me before men, I also will acknowledge before my Father who is in heaven, but whoever denies me before men, I also will deny before my Father who is in heaven" (Matt. 10:32-33). The faithful child of God abides in the teaching he received at the beginning of his walk. They have known the truth since the beginning of their Christian walk.

TRUTH ABIDES IN THEM: The truth we learned when we came to faith in

Christ Jesus must take up a permanent dwelling place in our hearts. When it does, then we will be able to abide in the Son and in the Father. Then we will receive the promise of *eternal life*. The apostle John often provided assurance about Jesus' Deity in this epistle. He did so in order to destroy the false teaching of the antichrists. The truth empowers us by giving us confidence that what the apostles and biblical writers said about Jesus was true. Don't fall for the lies of any religious teacher who changes the gospel message. The reward for faithfulness is eternal life.

MORE ON THE ANOINTING

> I write these things to you about those who are trying to deceive you. But the anointing that you received from him abides in you, and you have no need that anyone should teach you. But as his anointing teaches you about everything, and is true, and is no lie—just as it has taught you, abide in him.
>
> 1 John 2:26-27

John now denounces the antichrists as deceivers. The Greek word for deceiver is *planao* meaning "to make to wander, to lead astray". He also re-emphasizes the anointing we received from the Holy One, (Holy Spirit). Notice that the anointing abides in you and teaches you. We are told that the anointing will put us in a position where we do not need for anyone to teach us. Why? Because we have already been taught the truth and that truth abides in us. Perhaps that is what Jesus meant when he said "you will know the truth and the truth will set you free" (John 8:32).

We have already seen that the anointing refers to the indwelling of the Holy Spirit. Many New Testament passages teach us that the Holy Spirit dwells in us (Acts 2:38, 1 Cor. 3:16-17; 6:19-20). Ephesians 1:13-14 informs us that the Holy Spirit seals us and is the guarantee of our inheritance.

The Spirit, Himself, is our anointing. Every word the Spirit gave is true and not a lie. This is what we have been taught. Abide in that word. The inspired scriptures will equip us to discern between truth and error. Abide in Him (the Holy Spirit). After all, He abides in *us*!

RIGHTEOUSNESS

> And now, little children, abide in him, so that when he appears we may have confidence and not shrink from him at his coming. 29If you know that he is righteous, you may be sure that everyone who practices righteousness has been born of him.
>
> 1 John 2:28-29

For the third time John addresses his readers as little children. It is a term of endearment and not a criticism. In comparison to the apostle, they are still children spiritually. They need to grow as we all do. The children are encouraged to abide in him. How do we do that? We do so by believing and following the truth.

John now speaks of the second coming of Christ. Abide comes from the Greek word, "meno" meaning "to remain, dwell, to wait for." We are to abide in him so that "we may have confidence and not shrink from him at his coming." The King James Version says, "we may have confidence, and not be ashamed before him at his coming." Knowledge of the truth will give us great confidence when we see the Lord coming in His glory. We will not "shrink" from Him at His coming. To shrink means to be ashamed. We look forward to Jesus' coming because we know what a wonderful day that will be!

We also know that Jesus is righteous. We now learn that those who practice righteousness have also been born of Him. The Greek word "righteousness" is defined as "the doing or being what is just and right; the character and acts of a man commanded by and approved of God." I often tell people that righteousness "is to do what is right by God's standard." According to Romans 4:3, "Abraham believed God, and it was counted to him as righteousness." Our righteousness is imputed to us because of our faith. It is not given because of our goodness.

Abraham teaches us about righteousness. It was not that he deserved to be pronounced as righteous. It was because of his unfailing faith. Abraham believed God so much that "no distrust made him waver concerning the promise of God but he grew strong in his faith as he gave glory to God, fully convinced that God was able to do what he had promised" (Rom. 4:20-22). Abraham's righteousness was credited to him by his faith. Yes, we must keep God's commandments. However, it is only if we live by faith that God will declare us to be righteous. Those who practice righteousness have been born of God.

DISCUSSION QUESTIONS:

1. What does antichrist mean? Who were the antichrists of 1 John?
2. List three proofs that show us Jesus will not come back to earth to reign for 1,000 years?
3. Discuss the lesson about antichrist from 1 John 2:18-19.
4. What were two things the antichrists were saying about Jesus in 1 John 2:20-23.
5. How does it help us to abide in what we heard from the beginning?
6. Discuss the anointing we received when we became a Christian. Who gives it and what is it?
7. Discuss righteousness from 1 John 2:28-29.

CHAPTER SIX

REFRAINING FROM SIN

1 JOHN 3:1-10

LOVE PROVIDES MORAL BALANCE

> See what kind of love the Father has given to us, that we should be called children of God; and so we are. The reason why the world does not know us is that it did not know him.
>
> 1 John 3:1

This chapter reveals the need for believers to refrain from sin. However, instead of launching immediately into the topic we are reminded that those who believe are the objects of God's love. It is a special love likened unto that of a father for his beloved children. In 1 John 3:1-3 we are encouraged to open our eyes and see the love God has for His children. This love provides moral balance for our lives and prompts us to purify ourselves even as He is pure. The evidence of His love is seen by the fact that God is our Father and we are His children. How awesome is that?

The blessing of God's love is something to be enjoyed from the very moment we obey the Gospel. John said, "Beloved, we *are* God's children." John is telling us that we are His family *now*. Yes, it is true. His love and our family status is something to be enjoyed at this very moment. It is not something that is relegated to the far distant future.

Unfortunately, people in the world, who are outside of Christ, cannot fathom this family concept because they do not know the teachings found in the Bible. Far too many people claim to know God but their lifestyle declares they really don't know Him at all.

According to the Gospel of John a person cannot know God unless he knows Jesus (John 14:8-11). The only reliable source for learning about Jesus is the Bible. Jesus asked Philip, "Have I been with you so long, and you still do not know me, Philip? Whoever has seen me has seen the Father. How can you say, 'Show me the Father'" (John 14:9). When you look closely at Jesus you will not only get to know Him but you will also get to know our Heavenly Father. The strong Christian has a compelling desire to know more about Jesus. Consequently he is willing to do everything in his power to achieve that goal. The serendipity is this: When we learn more about Jesus we also learn more about God.

WHAT WE SHALL BE

> Beloved, we are God's children now, and what we will be has not yet appeared; but we know that when he appears we shall be like him because we shall see him as he is.
>
> 1 John 3:2

It is helpful for us to realize that we are God's children right now. It is not something we hope for in the future. We became His children the moment we obeyed the Gospel. While we can understand that we are God's family it is much more difficult for us to grasp how things will be in the future. Paul wrote about the second coming of Jesus in 1 Thessalonians 4:13-18. On that day Jesus will appear in the sky and the dead will be raised from the grave. Their bodies will be changed and they will meet Jesus in the air. Then the living will receive a resurrection body of their own and they will also go to meet the Lord in the air. Believers in the Bible know this will happen and they believe it is true. However, it is very difficult for us to grasp what kind of body we will receive. Until Jesus returns all we know about our resurrection body is this: When Christ appears we will be like Him.

In 1 Corinthians 15:35-49 we learn that first-century believers also had questions about the resurrection body. They asked Paul. "How are the dead raised? With what kind of body do they appear?" The Apostle Paul considered it to be a foolish question. Nevertheless, he gave them an inspired answer. The apostle pointed out that there are different kinds of flesh in the animal world. There are also different degrees of brightness in the heavenly lights. There is also a difference between our earthly bodies and our heavenly bodies. This question is further answered by showing us that our mortal body is sown a perishable body but it will be raised an imperishable body. Our resurrection body will be like the body of the resurrected Lord.

John, himself, said he did not know what the resurrection body would be like. If John didn't know the answer then neither do we. While we might yearn for additional information we must be content with the amount of information God chose to reveal to us. That is enough for me! I don't care what my resurrection body will be like. I just know that I want one! I also know for certain – that if I am faithful I *will* get one!

HOPE PROMPTS PURITY

> And everyone who thus hopes in him purifies himself as he is pure.
>
> 1 John 3:3

How does "hope" and "purity" fit into our study? First of all, let's consider the word "hope". The Greek word means the "expectation of something future."

One of my bible teachers taught me that hope is "desire plus expectation." It relates to promises yet to come. Our hope is not "pie in the sky" hope. It is the full expectation that God will do *everything* He promised to do.

The by-product of hope is purity. The word "pure" is from the Greek word "hagnos" and means "chaste, clean, not contaminated by anything in itself really evil . . . pure from every defilement." It is the Christian's fervent desire to keep himself pure even as Jesus is pure. Allow your hope to motivate you to live a pure lifestyle! The reward to be received will be well worth the effort.

REFRAINING FROM SIN

After hearing how much God loves us and after learning how much He wants to bless us we should be feeling a wonderful glow of satisfaction. We certainly should have a renewed hope that we will receive all of the wonderful promises of God. However, after bringing us to new heights of expectation, John begins a discussion on the need to refrain from sin.

Why must we go from our delightful study describing our hope to see Jesus as He is into a detailed discussion on sin? The reason is: When a child of God lives in a habitually sinful condition he loses God's favor. Unless we turn from the practice of sin we will lose our reward. It is important to know that God's promises are conditional.

The tragedy of sin is that it separates a person from God (Isa. 59:1-2). Even the blind man, who was healed by Jesus in John chapter nine, understood this truth. He said, "We know that God does not listen to sinners, but if anyone is a worshipper of God and does his will, God listens to him" (John 9:31).

EXAMINING THE SIN PROBLEM

Before studying the text of 1 John 3:4-10 we are going to examine the most common words used to describe sin. The Greek word translated "sin" means "to miss the mark". This word can be used to describe all kinds of wrongdoing. However, there are other words in the Bible that also describe sinful actions.

1. **SIN:** As already stated, the word sin means to "miss the mark". Everyone old enough to know right from wrong has been guilty of sin (Rom. 3:23).
2. **LAWLESSNESS:** meaning "contempt of law" (1 John 3:4). The idea is to contemptuously break the law of God.
3. **INIQUITY:** This word is defined in the lexicons as "Perversity" and is translated iniquities in Isaiah 59:1-2.
4. **TRANSGRESSION:** The primary meaning of this word is to "go across or pass over." In Matthew 15:2-3 the ESV uses the word "break" for the word that is usually translated transgression. The idea of transgression is to go too far or to cross over the line. Second John 9 translates the word with the phrase, "goes on ahead." Simply put, to transgress is to go too far.
5. **HUMAN WISDOM:** This sin occurs when men determine right or wrong based upon human standards (Prov. 16:25).
6. **FAILURE TO DO WHAT IS RIGHT:** This is a failure to do what we know is the right thing to do (Jas. 4:17).
7. **WRONGDOING:** The standard for doing right is God's word. All wrongdoing is sin (1 John 5:17). The word "wrongdoing" demonstrates that men who know God's word do have the ability to know when they have done something wrong. They have come to understand that all wrongdoing is sin.
8. **BLASPHEMY OF THE HOLY SPIRIT:** This is an unforgiveable sin. The Greek word translated blasphemy is defined as "slander." This sin occurs when a person claims that Jesus did His miracles by the power of the prince of demons or by an evil spirit rather than by the Holy Spirit. Read

> Mark 3:22-30 to learn more about this sin. An explanation of the blasphemy of the Holy Spirit is clearly stated in Mark 3:30. "For they said, He has an unclean spirit." Therefore anyone who says Jesus performed miracles by the power of an unclean spirit has committed a sin that will never be forgiven. Why? Because they have slandered Jesus by claiming He was empowered by the devil rather than by the Holy Spirit. Such a person cannot be forgiven because by denying the source of Jesus' power they also deny Jesus, the only begotten Son of God.

Everyone who has reached the age of maturity is able to determine right from wrong and will become guilty of sin. It is just a matter of time. Since this level of maturity differs with each individual we call it the "age of accountability." The Bible clearly states, "For all have sinned" (Rom. 3:23). No one is exempt from sinning except Jesus Christ our Lord.

REFUSE TO PRACTICE SIN

Now we are ready to look at the dangers of practicing sin (1 John 3:4-10). This passage provides us with a detailed discussion of sin and ends up by telling us that a person who is born of God does not practice sin. However, just because we have obeyed the Gospel of Christ does not mean that we are immune from sinning. Keeping our lives free from wrongdoing is a constant struggle for all of us. However, God promised us that we will not be tempted above our ability to endure. The Lord also promised to "provide the way of escape that you may be able to endure it" (1 Cor. 10:12-13). Be encouraged. God is always faithful to provide us with an escape route so that we need not fall into sin.

WHAT SIN IS: "Everyone who makes a practice of sinning also practices lawlessness, sin is lawlessness" (1 John 3:4). You must realize that John is speaking of one who sins habitually. This person is making no effort to stop his wrongdoing.

Such a one will be condemned because he continues doing sinful things. This type of sinner is called a lawless person. Even if he attends every worship service and says all of the right things, his habitual sins stand between him and God (Isa. 59:1-2). Examine yourself often in order to stay aware of your shortcomings. Do your very best not to commit the same sins over and over again without making any effort to repent.

WHAT SIN DEMANDED: "You know that he appeared to take away sins, and in him there is no sin" (1 John 3:5). Simply put, our sins demanded a perfect sacrifice. Jesus made the only sacrifice acceptable to God when he died on the cross. Christ shed His blood in order to pay the price for our sins. "For our sake he made him to be sin who knew no sin, so that in him we might become the righteousness of God" (2 Corinthians 5:21). Our sins require a price we cannot pay. Thank you, God, for sending Jesus to earth. He paid the price for all of us!

Our Father made a plan to save sinful man before He created the world (Eph. 1:4; 1 Pet. 1:18-21). Under the Law of Moses animal sacrifices were required for the sins of Israel. The priests were commanded to shed the blood of a flawless animal as a sacrifice for sin. However, they did not realize the weakness of their offerings. The Bible clearly says, "it is impossible for the blood of bulls and goats to take away sin" (Heb. 10:4). Sacrifices made under the Law were only a shadow of what Jesus would accomplish for us on the cross. Only the precious blood of Jesus was able to do that. Thank you, Jesus, for making such a great sacrifice on behalf of all mankind. Thank you, Jesus, for making that sacrifice for *me*!

WHY SIN EXISTS: "No one who abides in him keeps on sinning; no one who keeps on sinning has either seen him or known him" (1 John 3:6). Why does sin exist? Sin exists because of human weakness. We fall so easily for the devil's temptations. It is not because of the sin of Adam that we are sinners – it is because of our own sins. "The soul who sins shall die" (Ezek. 18:20).

However, just because we have such a propensity to sin does not mean we have no choice in the matter. God's desire for us is that we do not sin. When a person makes his permanent dwelling place in God he is certainly less likely to sin. For sure, his heart will not allow him to habitually commit the same sins over and over again. His tender heart will bring him to repentance and lead him back to godly living. That is why John wrote, "No one who abides in him keeps on sinning". It is the goal of the righteous to get out of the sinning business altogether. It is his goal to live a holy life that is acceptable to God.

Tragically, anyone who keeps on sinning has neither seen nor known God. Read the tragic history of Israel from the time they left Egypt through the book of Malachi, a period of about 1,000 years. Most of the Israelites knew God's name, Jehovah, but they did not know Him. They had received His law but they did not obey it. They made animal sacrifices but not with holy hands. Their offerings to God were not acceptable because they were living perpetually sinful lives while making no effort to change their evil ways. They did not spend enough time thinking about God and His commandments. "My people have forgotten me days without number" (Jer. 2:32).

Believers must strive to be a holy people. God commanded us to do so. "As obedient children do not be conformed to the passions of your former ignorance, but as he who called you is holy you also must be holy in all your conduct, since it is written, You shall be holy for I am holy" (1 Pet. 1:14-16). When will we learn to live in the world but not be of the world? When will we learn to resist the devil so that he will flee from us (Jas. 4:7)? In 1 John 3:6 two clear truths are revealed.

1. The person who abides in Him does not continue in sin. Oh yes, there will be isolated acts of sin. But the child of God readily acknowledges his sins before God and he refuses to practice the same sins habitually without making any effort to get right with God.
2. The person who keeps on sinning has neither seen nor known God. He sins without any thought of repentance or reform.

Can you see the difference in the two points above? Can you see how the mature child of God makes every effort to keep from sinning?

THE ORIGIN OF SIN: "Little children, let no one deceive you. Whoever practices righteousness is righteous, as he is righteous. Whoever makes a practice of sinning is of the devil, for the devil has been sinning from the beginning" (1 John 3:7-8). Now we learn the simple truth that people who practice righteousness are righteous even as He is righteous. By faith in Him we are declared to be righteous (Gal. 3:6). This declaration is not by our own goodness but by the goodness of Christ. "He is our righteousness" (1 Cor. 1:30).

Knowledge of God, through the word, will not allow the faithful child of God to continue in sin. When he does do something wrong he feels the pain so deeply that he repents. It then becomes his firm determination to never commit that sin again. Righteousness is his goal and his desire. For that reason he will not, no, he cannot continue in sin. He strives to be a faithful servant of the Lord every day of his life.

The person who habitually practices sin is of the devil. The devil has been sinning from the beginning. The fall of man, as recorded in Genesis 3, clearly demonstrates that the devil is an evil slanderer whose goal is to lead people away from God. The word, "devil" comes from the Greek word "diabolos" meaning "false accuser, slanderer." Our "first couple" began their lives without sin. It does not appear that they remained sinless for very long.

Eve fell for the devil's lies and ate of the forbidden fruit. Adam was not deceived by the falsehood but he ate anyway (1 Tim. 2:14). On that very day, at the very moment they sinned, they both died. They died a spiritual death as demanded by the Law of Sin and Death (Rom. 8:2). This law requires the soul that sins must die. Thanks be to God that the Law of Sin and Death lost its power through the work of Jesus Christ our Lord.

In John 8:39-47, Jesus told the sinful Jewish leaders they were of their father the devil. As expected, they denied Jesus' words and claimed to be children of

Abraham. The Jewish leader's denial of Jesus proved they were not doing what Abraham did. The Lord said to them, "You are of your father the devil, and your will is to do your father's desires . . . When he lies, he speaks out of his own character, for he is a liar and the father of lies" (John 8:44). We must face the truth that every sin we commit, whether it be through improper actions, words, or thoughts comes to us through the temptations of the devil. John put it this way, "Whoever makes a practice of sinning is of the devil." He is the originator of sin and he wants to destroy every one of us just like he tried to do with Adam and Eve.

Consider this contrast. The origin of sin is the devil, a sinner from before the beginning of time. The origin of salvation is God through His Son Jesus. Even though Joshua was an Old Testament leader he gave good advice when he said, "Choose you this day whom you will serve . . . as for me and my house, we will serve the Lord" (Josh. 24:15). Joshua made a good choice. Follow that godly man's advice and refuse to commit habitual sins. Choose to serve God and follow His commandments and – do it right now!

THOSE BORN OF GOD DO NOT PRACTICE SINNING: "No one born of God makes a practice of sinning, for God's seed abides in him, and he cannot keep on sinning because he has been born of God. By this it is evident who are the children of God, and who are the children of the devil: whoever does not practice righteousness is not of God, nor is the one who does not love his brother" (1 John 3:9-10). John made some bold statements in this passage as he explained some important reasons why the child of God can not make it his practice to keep on sinning.

First of all, John wrote "No one born of God makes a practice of sinning." That is because he is born of God and His seed is in him. This believer made a personal commitment not to make it a practice of sinning. The phrase "practice of sinning" speaks of one who habitually commits the same sin over and over again. The person who is born of God does not behave that way. When he sins his conscience will not allow him to continue to commit that sin. John clearly said, "He cannot keep on sinning because he has been born of God."

Children of God practice righteousness (v. 10). A person's lifestyle makes it evident whether he is a child of God or a child of the devil. The contrast is easy to detect. The child of the devil does not practice righteousness. Neither does he love his brother. The child of God does both.

Children of God love their brothers (v. 10). The final sentence in this verse transitions to the topic of brotherly love. This important topic will be the central topic of 1 John 3:11-24. For this reason, the next chapter in this book is called Love's Compelling Nature.

The child of God is able to refrain from sin by his knowledge of the scriptures. His knowledge must be coupled with the desire to be righteous. When you put enough of the word of God into your heart and when you have enough love for God to follow his commandments, then you will be able to refrain from habitually committing the same sins over and over again. Instead, you will become a shining light to the living by being an example of godly living.

DISCUSSION QUESTIONS:

1. Define the word "hope." Discuss ways we can have more hope.
2. Who are the "children" spoken of in 1 John 3:1? Name the evidences that we are objects of God's love.
3. Explain the different kinds of sins mentioned in our discussion of 1 John 3:4-10.
4. Discuss the following headings that help us to better understand the sin problem: 1) What sin is, 2) What sin demanded, 3) Why sin exists, 4) The origin of sin, and 5) Those who conquer sin.
5. Discuss the man who conquers sin (1 John 4:9-10).

CHAPTER SEVEN

LOVE'S COMPELLING NATURE

1 JOHN 3:11-24

THE IMPERATIVE OF LOVE

> For this is the message that you have heard from the beginning, that we should love one another.
>
> 1 John 3:11

Fifty-two times John uses the word love in his epistles. This section presents the compelling nature of love. God's message for all believers is to "love one another." This commandment includes loving sinners as well as the faithful. We will see this theme over and over again in the remainder of our study of John's epistles. Love is especially prominent in 1 John 4. Perhaps this is why many call John the apostle of love. Of course, he is not the only one to speak on the topic. Paul penned 1 Corinthians 13:1-13, a great chapter on love. Paul summed up his discussion on love with the following statement: "So now faith, hope, and love abide, these three, but the greatest of these is love" (1 Cor. 13:13).

What is love? The Greek word "agape" is translated by the English word love. Bullinger's *Critical Lexicon and Concordance* defines love as follows: "agape denotes the love which springs from admiration and veneration, and which chooses its object with decision of will, and denotes self-denying and compassionate devotion to it." It is love in its fullest form. I have often heard it said that love is to consider another person's highest good.

Verse 11 presents the first part of John's teaching on love. It is the imperative of love. It has been commanded from the beginning and is something we must do. You might argue that some people are really not very loveable. That argument just won't do. Loving one another is not something we are unable to accomplish. Otherwise God would not have commanded us to do it. Love is an imperative. We cannot follow God without it. Later we will learn that we cannot even love God if we do not love our brother.

HUMAN NATURE DEFINED BY CAIN

> We should not be like Cain, who was of the evil one and murdered his brother. And why did he murder him? Because his own deeds were evil and his brother's righteous. Do not be surprised, brothers, that the world hates you. We know that we have passed out of death into life, because we love the brothers. Whoever does not love abides in death. Everyone who hates his brother is a murderer, and you know that no murderer has eternal life abiding in him.
>
> 1 John 3:12-15

Before extolling Christian love John presents the hateful actions of Cain as a warning to those who hate their brothers. WARNING! Do not be like Cain. You might want to read Genesis chapter four to refresh your memory on the events that caused Cain to murder his brother, Abel. John knew it was a familiar story so he summarized the events. Cain was of the evil one, the devil. He hated his brother and ended up killing him. Don't be surprised if the world hates you. Evil always hates righteousness.

1. Why did Cain murder his brother? Because his deeds were evil while Abel's were righteous.
2. The wicked hate the righteous. "I have given them your word, and the world has hated them because they are not of the world, just as I am not of the world" (John 17:14). Don't be surprised if the world hates YOU!
3. The righteous pass from death into life. This statement speaks of our conversion (Rom. 6:1-7; 10:12-17). However, in spite of our best efforts it is sometimes difficult to do the right thing and love our brothers. Let's face it. Some people are more difficult to love than others. I am reminded of Romans chapter seven where Paul decries his inability to do the good things he wanted to do. He lamented his failures and attributed them to sin that dwelled in him. "I do not understand my own actions. For I do not do what I want, but I do the very thing I hate" (Rom. 7:15). Paul concludes with the cry "Wretched man that I am! Who will deliver me from this body of death?" (Rom. 7:24). The answer is, "Thanks be to God, through Jesus Christ our Lord" (Rom. 7:25). Through Him we can be righteous and we can follow Him. Heed the warning: *Do not be like Cain*! Love your brothers and you will have life.
4. Cain was guilty of three sins. First, his offering was not of faith. We know that "faith comes from hearing and hearing through the word of Christ" (Rom. 10:17). Therefore we can rightly conclude that God told Cain what to offer but he disobeyed. His second sin was to murder his brother. The third sin of Cain was lying to God in an effort to hide his sin (Gen. 4:8-9). "Everyone who hates his brother is a murderer and no murderer has eternal life abiding in him" (1 John 3:15). It is frightening to learn that if we hate our brother we are a murderer! Such a person cannot inherit eternal life. *Do not be like Cain*!

There is another side to this story. When we sin we have the opportunity to begin anew. We can pass out of spiritual death into life. This is made possible by brotherly love. Yes, that is exactly what John teaches. "We know that we have passed out of death into life, because we love the brothers. Whoever does not love abides in death. Everyone who hates his brother is a murderer, and you know that no murderer has eternal life abiding in him" (1 John 3:14-15).

Do you see the process?

1. Because we love our brothers we pass from death into life.
2. Without love we abide in spiritual death.
3. No murderer has eternal life abiding in him. Whoever hates his brother is a murderer already. Such a person does not have eternal life abiding in him. The importance of brotherly love cannot be overly stated.

FOUR IMPORTANT STEPS

> By this we know love, that he laid down his life for us, and we ought to lay down our lives for the brothers. But if anyone has the world's goods and sees his brother in need, yet closes his heart against him, how does God's love abide in him? Little children, let us not love in word or talk but in deed and in truth.
>
> 1 John 3:16-18

First of all we will explore four helpful steps that will assist us in understanding Godlike love.

STEP ONE: Realize the love Jesus had for us, a love that caused Him to lay down His life on our behalf. That is the ultimate sacrifice. The Lord Jesus died for us even though we were totally unworthy of His sacrifice. Read Romans 5:6-9 for more on what Jesus did for us while we were still sinners.

STEP TWO: In response to Jesus' sacrifice for us we must be willing to lay down our own life for our brothers. It is one thing to nod our heads in "approval" for what Jesus did on our behalf. The real test is whether we are willing to lay down our lives for others.

This could mean physically dying for a brother. However, it is more likely speaking of giving our lives in service to others. What have you given of yourself in service to your brothers lately? Was your deed a loving sacrifice or just a "duty" you felt you had to do?

STEP THREE: This step provides a test of our brotherly love. The test is our willingness to sharing our worldly goods with those in need? (1 John 3:17-18). When we close our hearts to the physical needs of others we are providing evidence that the love of God does not abide in us. The first-century church willingly sacrificed their physical belongings with those in need (Acts 2:44-45; 24:17). "As we have opportunity let us do good to everyone, and especially to those who are of the household of faith" (Galatians 6:10). Read James 2:14-18 for another example of believers helping those in need. The New Testament is filled with examples of God's people sharing their physical goods with those in need. How can we do any less today?

STEP FOUR: Love is not just talk. Love shows itself in deed and in truth. The early Christians did so well in the area of sacrificial giving that there was no one in the congregation who lacked the necessities of life. The first-century church practiced brotherly love in a powerful way as they sold their lands and goods in order to share the proceeds with those in need. Read Acts 4:32-37 for a wonderful example of loving self-sacrifice in action. Love is not talk – it is action!

THE VALUE OF LOVE

> By this we shall know that we are of the truth and reassure our heart before him; for whenever our heart condemns us, God is greater than our heart, and he knows everything. Beloved, if our heart does not condemn us, we have confidence before God;

> and whatever we ask we receive from him, because we keep his commandments and do what pleases him. And this is his commandment, that we believe in the name of his Son Jesus Christ and love one another, just as he has commanded us. Whoever keeps his commandments abides in God, and God in him. And by this we know that he abides in us, by the Spirit whom he has given us.
>
> 1 John 3:19-24

It is always reassuring to know we are of the truth. We can only be of the truth when we know truth and follow it. In this context, the truth under consideration is brotherly love. Such knowledge gives us assurance and it also sets us free from self-condemnation. When we love each other our heart doesn't condemn us and we have confidence before God. That is because we are practicing brotherly love.

However, there are times when our heart does condemn us. When we fail to love each other our self-condemnation is justified. Granted, there are times when we are being too hard on ourselves. We must never forget that God is the judge of our hearts and He knows everything about us (Psa. 139). God knows when we love Him and our brothers. God has knowledge of our deepest thoughts and attitudes. God knows whether or not we keep His commandments from the heart. Such a person abides in Him. Our heavenly Father also abides in us through the Holy Spirit he gave us.

God's commandments are many but the specific commandments under consideration in 1 John 3:23, are to believe in Jesus Christ and to love one another. Don't make the mistake of thinking these are the only commandments we have to keep because there are certainly others to keep. However these two are high on God's list. John reminds us to believe in the name of Jesus Christ and to obey His commandments. Jesus once asked the question, "Why do you call me Lord, Lord, and not do what I tell you" (Luke 6:46)? Jesus also commanded us to "love one another." Doing what Jesus commands us to do proves that we abide in God and that He abides in us.

Someone might ask, "How do I know for sure that He abides in me?" John anticipated that question in 1 John 3:24. "And by this we know that he abides in us, by the Spirit whom he has given us." The indwelling of the Holy Spirit of God in the Christian is positive proof that we abide in Him and He in us.

1. The Spirit was promised to those who believed in Jesus (John 7:38-39). When Jesus spoke these words He was promising the indwelling of the Spirit as a blessing that would come to obedient believers in the Christian age.
2. In Acts 2:38 Peter promised the 3,000 who were baptized on the Day of Pentecost that they would receive "the gift of the Holy Spirit." That gift is the Holy Spirit Himself. He dwells in everyone who obeys the gospel. Jesus promised to give the Spirit and when the church began He kept His promise.
3. Paul wrote that the Holy Spirit was given to believers as the guarantee of their inheritance (Eph. 1:13-14). He also taught that our bodies are the temple of the Holy Spirit who is "within you." The knowledge of the indwelling of the Holy Spirit is clearly stated by Paul in 1 Corinthians 3:16-17; 6:19-20. Certainly, the bible provides an abundance of proof that the Holy Spirit abides in the child of God. It is something that we can know for sure (1 John 3:24).

The emphasis of this chapter is love. We are to love our brothers even as Jesus loves us. Love is extremely important to the child of God. We love God, we love Jesus, and we love each other. To give us more confidence, the Lord gave us His Holy Spirit to dwell in us.

DISCUSSION QUESTIONS:

1. What do we learn about Cain in 1 John 3:12-15?
2. What do we learn about brotherly love in 1 John 3:12-15?
3. Who is the evil one? Why did Cain murder Abel?
4. Discuss the four steps concerning brotherly love from 1 John 3:16-18.
5. List the three sins of Cain.
6. What does it mean to "pass from death into life"?
7. What does it mean when the Bible says, "he abides in us by the Spirit whom he has given us" (1 John 3:2)?
8. Discuss the indwelling of the Holy Spirit. What does it mean to you?

CHAPTER EIGHT

KNOWING THE SPIRIT OF TRUTH

1 JOHN 4:1-6

TEST THE SPIRITS

> Beloved, do not believe every spirit, but test the spirits to see whether they are from God, for many false prophets have gone out into the world.
>
> 1 John 4:1

This is the fourth time John calls believers "beloved." See the comments on 1 John 2:7-8 for a more complete description of the term. Do you find it strange that John would begin a section on false prophets with the word "beloved"? Maybe he is appealing to the loving relationship between John and the ones to whom he wrote. They were dear to him and John did not want them to be led astray by false prophets who claimed to be God's servants. To be called beloved should thrill one's soul.

Immediately after this warm introduction the apostle gives a stern warning to "test the spirits to see whether they are from God, for many false prophets have gone out into the world." When we listen to a sermon, read a book, or listen to a biblical discussion we must make our very best effort to test the message we are learning against the word of God. Only in this way can we determine whether the teaching is true or false. The word "test" is from the Greek word "dokimazo" meaning "make trial of, put to the proof, examine, as metals by fire, to prove, try." We test the spirits by contrasting what we hear from men with what the Bible teaches. This will reveal to us what is true and what is error.

In every age there have been false teachers. John instructs us to be careful whom we believe because there have been, and always will be, many false prophets in the world. Since his advice is timeless it is applicable to every generation. We will now spend a bit of time examining different kinds of false prophets found in the Bible. We will use the term prophet to include all who teach and preach the word of God. This lesson includes those who teach God's word in this present age.

EXAMPLES FROM THE OLD TESTAMENT

THOSE WHO DO NOT KNOW JEHOVAH: In the Old Testament the downfall of Israel came because they turned to the gods of the land. In truth, these gods were the product of man's imagination and were not gods at all. The idol worshippers did not know Jehovah. All manmade idols were to be rejected by God's faithful people. Jehovah, in His wrath, punished everyone who worshipped idols. Will He do any differently today?

ELIJAH THE PROPHET: Consider the contest between the prophet Elijah and the 450 prophets of Baal (1 Kings 18). This was a contest between the one true God and the pagan god Baal. Ahab was the King of Israel and was married to a foreign woman named Jezebel. She worshipped the god Baal and turned her husband into a follower of that idolatrous religion. After a long drought, Elijah challenged the Baal prophets to a contest. He said, "How long will you go limping between two different opinions? If the Lord is God, follow him; but if Baal, then follow him" (1 Kings 18:21).

The challenge was for the prophets of Baal and Elijah to have a contest to prove who was the one true God. They were to place a sacrifice on the altar and pray for their Deity to provide the fire. The prophets of Baal worked long and hard but failed to succeed. That is because Baal is not God. About the time of the evening sacrifice, Elijah dug a trench around the altar he had built, drenched it with water and prayed to God. Fire immediately came down from heaven and lapped up the water and burned the sacrifice. The people rounded up the prophets of Baal and Elijah put them to death at the brook Kishon. The people saw clear and plain evidence that Baal was not a god but that Jehovah was God. That day a great victory was won. A total of 450 false prophets of Baal were slain that day.

If anyone presents a deity different from the God of the Bible we MUST reject that teacher. If you believe the Bible you must agree there is only one God. "Thus says the Lord, the King of Israel and his Redeemer, the Lord of hosts: I am the first and I am the last; besides me there is no god" (Isaiah 44:6). In verse 8 we read, "Is there a God besides me? There is no Rock; I know not any." We must "test the prophets to see whether they are from God."

JEREMIAH THE PROPHET: This prophet of God revealed three kinds of false prophets that were teaching in Israel. First, there were the false prophets who served the idolatrous gods of the Nations. Secondly, some of Israel's false prophets worshipped the gods of the land as well as Jehovah God. The Lord was NOT pleased when His people bowed down in worship to both the pagan idols and to Jehovah God. We do not have the right to serve multiple Gods. "You shall have no other gods before me" (Exod. 20:3). Thirdly, there were the false Israelite prophets who delivered messages that did not originate with God. Their messages came from their own deluded minds.

Consider God's warning to Israel when they followed the message of false prophets and served the gods of the land. "My people have forgotten me; they make offerings to false gods; they made them stumble in their ways, in the ancient roads, and to walk into side roads, not the highway . . .Like the east wind I will scatter them before the enemy. I will show them my back, not my face, in the day of their calamity" (Jer. 18:15; 17). There are serious consequences to face for anyone who serves any god other than Jehovah.

Take a look at how God felt about the false teachers in Israel. "Concerning the prophets: My heart is broken within me; all my bones shake; I am like a drunken man, like a man overcome by wine, because of the Lord and because of his holy words . . . Both prophet and priest are ungodly; even in my house I have found their evil, declares the Lord" (Jer. 23:9, 11). "I did not send the prophets, yet they ran; I did not speak to them, yet they prophesied. But if they had stood in my council, then they would have proclaimed my words to my people, and they would have turned them from their evil way, and from the evil of their deeds" (Jer. 23:21-22). Sadly, it breaks God's heart when mankind serves any god other that Jehovah Himself.

Now, hear the word of God concerning false prophets. "For thus says the Lord of hosts, the God of Israel: Do not let your prophets and diviners who are among you deceive you, and do not listen to the dreams that they dream, for it is a lie that they are prophesying to you in my name: I did not send them, declares the Lord" (Jer. 29:8-9). We must "test the prophets to see whether they are from God" (1 John 4:1).

NEW TESTAMENT TEACHERS

THE APOSTLE PETER: This apostle informs his readers that false prophets would be in existence during every generation. What was true in Peter's day is also true for us. Be warned: There are false teachers at work right now, today. They are following the pattern of the false teachers from years gone by. They "secretly bring in destructive heresies, even denying the Master who bought them, bringing upon themselves swift destruction. And many will follow their sensuality and because of them the way of truth will be blasphemed. And in their greed they will exploit you with false words. Their condemnation from long ago is not idle, and their destruction is not asleep" (2 Pet. 2:1-3).

Far too many people believe that anyone holding a Bible in his hand is a trustworthy spokesman for God. If they dress well, if they have a nice "spiritual environment" surrounding them and if they speak eloquently they are accepted as faithful. Please know that just because a person has the ability to flip through his bible and speak fluently does not guarantee his teaching is true. If we trust those who teach us to a level where we don't examine the Bible for ourselves we could easily be led astray. Even in the 21st century we must "test the prophets to see whether they are from God." Below are some types of teachers to avoid:

TEACHERS WHO LACK UNDERSTANDING: These are people who desire to be teachers of the word of God but they don't know what they are talking about. Paul wrote about them when he said, "Certain persons, by swerving from these, have wandered away into vain discussion, desiring to be teachers of the law, without understanding either what they are saying or the things about which they make confident assertions" (1 Tim. 1:6-7).

It is vital that we train our teachers in the word of God so they can teach accurately. "You then, my child, be strengthened by the grace that is in Christ Jesus and what you have heard from me in the presence of many witnesses entrust to faithful men who will be able to teach others also" (2 Tim. 2:1-2). Teachers without a proper understanding of the word will lead others astray unintentionally. They just don't have enough knowledge to teach accurately. Perhaps this is why James warned us with the following words. "Not many of you should become teachers, my brothers, for you know that we who teach will be judged with greater strictness" (Jas. 3:1). It is not that we need fewer teachers. What we need are learned teachers who are able to teach the word of God accurately.

It would be wise to follow the example given by the people who heard the word of God in the city of Berea. Even though they were listening to the great apostle Paul, a faithful teacher of the word, they felt it necessary to examine "the Scriptures daily to see if these things were so" (Acts 17:11). We all have an obligation to study for ourselves so that we can "test the prophets to see whether they are from God."

TEACHERS WITH IMPROPER MOTIVES: Second Peter 2 reveals some of the improper motives found in some Bible teachers.

1. There are teachers who bring in heresies, from a Greek word meaning "taking a choice; option, a preference, a chosen way or plan; a sect" (2 Pet. 2:1). In the book of 1 John the heretics were the antichrists who denied Jesus' Deity. Their teaching would lead to the destruction of both the teacher and those who accepted their words.
2. Some are greedy. They taught for the purpose of receiving excessive monetary gain. It is not wrong for evangelists to receive money for their work but it is wrong to teach others for the purpose of becoming rich (2 Pet. 2:3). Some teachers, like Balaam, forsook the right way. They loved gain from wrongdoing (2 Pet. 2:15). The apostle Paul adds, "The love of money is a root of all kinds of evils" (1 Tim. 6:10).
3. Some teachers promote ungodly lifestyles (2 Pet. 2:13). They participated in shameful actions. They "count it pleasure to revel in the daytime" because they had no shame.
4. Some practiced immorality having eyes for "adultery insatiable for sin . . . Accursed children" (2 Pet. 2:14). The Bible consistently teaches that immoral sexual activity is a sin. The same is true today!

SOMETIMES GOD TESTS US: In Deuteronomy 13:1-4 we learn that God tested Israel through teachings of the false prophets. God allowed these false prophets to tempt Israel to follow heathen gods. In this way God discovered if His people would remain faithful to Him or not. False prophets were to be put to death because they taught rebellion against the Lord (Deut. 13:5).

It is an amazing truth that God allowed these false prophets to teach falsehood as a test of faith for God's people. When His people followed the teaching of the false prophets they failed the test. Then God punished those who believed the teachings as well as the lying prophets. We must "test the prophets to see whether they are from God."

We have spent several pages discussing 1 John 4:1. Even so, I want to conclude this section with some quotations from Scripture that show just how God feels about false teachers. These verses are self-explanatory and do not need my comments. Consider them carefully.

A WARNING FROM GOD HIMSELF!

JEREMIAH 23:16: "Thus says the LORD of hosts: 'Do not listen to the words of the prophets who prophesy to you, filling you with vain hopes. They speak visions of their own minds, not from the mouth of the LORD.'"

JEREMIAH 23:21-22: "I did not send the prophets, yet they ran; I did not speak to them, yet they prophesied. But if they had stood in my council, then they would have proclaimed my words to my people, and they would have turned them from their evil way, and from the evil of their deeds."

DEUTERONOMY 18:20-22: "'But the prophet who presumes to speak a word in my name that I have not commanded him to speak, or who speaks in the name of other gods, that same prophet shall die.' And if you say in your heart, 'How may we know the word that the LORD has not spoken?'— when a prophet speaks in the name of the LORD, if the word does not come to pass or come true, that is a word that the LORD has not spoken; the prophet has spoken it presumptuously. You need not be afraid of him.'"

GALATIANS 1:6-9: "I am astonished that you are so quickly deserting him who called you in the grace of Christ and are turning to a different gospel— not that there is another one, but there are some who trouble you and want to distort the gospel of Christ. But even if we or an angel from heaven should preach to you a gospel contrary to the one we preached to you, let him be accursed. As we have said before, so now I say again: If anyone is preaching to you a gospel contrary to the one you received, let him be accursed."

We must test the teaching we receive from others against the word of God so that we may determine if it is true. That is necessary because there are many false prophets in the world. This presents us with a difficult task. However, God will help us to understand His word when we search for truth with a sincere heart and when we pray for the wisdom to properly understand it. "Look carefully then how you walk, not as unwise but as wise, making the best use of the time, because the days are evil. Therefore do not be foolish, but understand what the will of the Lord is" (Eph. 5:15-17).

A TEST FOR ALL WHO TEACH

> By this you know the Spirit of God: every spirit that confesses that Jesus Christ has come in the flesh is from God, and every spirit that does not confess Jesus is not from God. This is the spirit of the antichrist, which you heard was coming and now is in the world already. Little children, you are from God and have overcome them, for he who is in you is greater than he who is in the world.
>
> 1 John 4:2-4

The primary test for a teacher is whether or not his words come to pass. In addition, their words must not conflict with other clear and plain passages of scripture. The Holy Spirit was the one who inspired the writers of the Bible (2 Pet. 1:20-21). The words a teacher speaks demonstrate whether he is teaching the inspired words of the Spirit of God or just his own ideas. The knowledge of the Apostle John was quite different from that of the antichrists. Their teaching conflicted with other plain and clear passages of Scripture. Unfortunately, the doctrine of the antichrists was causing some of the believers to be deceived. It was turning some of the brethren away from the apostle's doctrine.

Once again John informs us that the antichrists were already in the world. He told us this information earlier in 1 John 2:18. These men were believers who taught falsehood in regard to the Deity of Christ. Notice their claims. They taught that Jesus Christ did not come in the flesh and they would not confess Jesus; which is likely a denial that Jesus was the Son of God. We are not talking about people outside of the church. John informs us that the teaching of the antichrists was not from God. The antichrists were not *for* Jesus – they were *against* Him.

The doctrine of the antichrists was from man and not from God. Evidently these teachers just could not wrap their minds around the idea that God, who existed from eternity, could (or would) empty Himself and be born in the flesh. However, according to the Bible, that is exactly what happened (Phil. 2:5-11). The antichrists took the world's view by considering it impossible for God to literally become flesh and bones. They spoke words that originated from the minds of men and the world listened to them. True believers would overcome the antichrists because they were from God and He who is in us is "greater than he who is in the world." The true believers are greater than the worldly false teachers because their knowledge originates from God and not from the world.

TRUE TEACHERS ARE FROM GOD

> They are from the world; therefore they speak from the world, and the world listens to them. We are from God. Whoever knows God listens to us; whoever is not from God does not listen to us. By this we know the Spirit of truth and the spirit of error.
>
> 1 John 4:5-6

The antichrists were from the world thus they spoke words of human wisdom. The problem is, "in the wisdom of God, the world did not know God through wisdom, it pleased God through the folly of what we preach to save those who believe" (1 Cor. 1:21). Teachers can appear to have great wisdom and logic but if their teaching conflicts with the words found in Scripture we must reject what they teach. The antichrists taught with great words of worldly wisdom. This caused many people to be receptive to them.

"We are from God." Who is the "we" from verse 6? It refers to the apostles and other inspired writers of the Bible. These men spoke and wrote words given to them by the Holy Spirit (John 14:25-26; 16:12-13). Some believe the "we" includes all of the faithful teachers in the church and that could be true. However, it seems more correct to me to hold the view it refers to the apostles and other inspired writers of the Bible. It is unwise to go beyond what is written (1 Cor. 4:6). We must compare our teacher's words with what is recorded in Scripture.

The "we are from God" in verse 6 stands in stark contrast to the teachings of the antichrists. "Whoever knows God listens to us, whoever is not from God does not listen to us. By this we know the Spirit of truth and the spirit of error." This sentence reveals to us how we can know the difference between truth and error. The Spirit of truth provided absolute truth to faithful men like the apostles. John said, "We are from God" (1 John 4:6). Any doctrine that contradicts the words of those faithful men can only be defined by the term "the spirit of error." We only have two choices: The Spirit of truth or the spirit of error. Which will you choose? Just know that we can know the difference between "the Spirit of truth and the spirit of error."

DISCUSSION QUESTIONS:

1. Look at the discussion entitled "TEST THE SPIRITS" and discuss some ways we can determine truth from error.
2. How did Elijah prove Jehovah was God? What happened to the false prophets?

3. List the three kinds of false prophets mentioned by Jeremiah.
4. In the section on New Testament Teachers, Peter reveals two kinds of teachers. Discuss them and be sure to include their improper motives in your discussion.
5. Discuss the amazing truth that God tested Israel through false prophets. Include the punishment for the false teachers and those who followed them.
6. What two errors were being taught by the antichrists in 1 John 4:1-3?

CHAPTER NINE

ABIDE IN GOD'S LOVE

1 JOHN 4:7-21

LOVE IS EVIDENCE WE KNOW GOD

> Beloved, let us love one another, for love is from God, and whoever loves has been born of God and knows God. Anyone who does not love does not know God, because God is love.
>
> 1 John 4:7-8

This section further develops the need for us to practice brotherly love, an action that proves we know God. John makes his own love for the brethren evident when he calls them "beloved" for the fifth time. The word "beloved" will appear a sixth time in 1 John 4:11. Have you ever heard anyone use the term "beloved" when addressing a fellow believer? Think how you might address one of your fellow Christians by the word. When you do, you can expect a shocked look or, at least, a look of surprise from the one upon whom you bestowed this loving word of endearment.

First John 4:7 reveals to us that love is from God. He is the source. Without Him there is no godly love. Without Him, the only love in existence would be the sensuous and ungodly love found in an unbelieving world. Far too many look at love as nothing more than the gratification of sexual urges. God's love is defined as that which seeks the other person's highest good.

This kind of love comes only from God. It is not difficult to grasp the meaning of verses 7-8. Brotherly love proves we have been born of God and it shows that we know Him. Love comes from God because God is love.

LOVE ONE ANOTHER: Far too many people only love those who love them. No doubt we all have special people whom we love dearly. Those people are special to us and it is very easy for us to love them. Then there are others that are more difficult for us to love. However, we must learn how to love "unlovable" people too. The command is to love one another. That means everybody! This is not to say that we cannot have people who are especially close to us. John called himself "the disciple whom Jesus loved" (John 21:20). That does not mean our Lord did not love the other apostles.

It should be easy for a child of God to love his fellow believers because they are family members. Well-rounded families are able to love every single member of the family with their whole heart. We must keep in mind that the church is God's family. We cannot pick and choose whom we will love. God expects us to love everyone in the family! No excuses! Just do it!

It is much more difficult for us to love sinners. That is because their sinful lifestyle makes it easy for us to hate the sinner as well as his transgressions. However, from John 3:16 we learn that God so loved the world that He sent His Son to save us. This includes all of the people (good or bad) who live in this old world. Sometimes it is difficult for us to separate a person from his sinful actions. However, we can do it. God would not give us commandments to keep that we do not have the ability to obey. If we don't love the lost we will NOT be motivated to carry out the Great Commission. Take a moment to meditate on what the commandment to love one another means. Then see if there is anything you can do that will help you do a better job of carrying out this very important commandment.

LOVE IS FROM GOD: The source of love is God Himself. When our heavenly Father created the human race He placed certain godly characteristics within us. Among those attributes is the ability to love others. The ability to love comes from God because God is love. When we understand that God loves even "unlovable me" it will help us to develop the ability to love others.

When a family has a newborn child it is only natural for the parents and all of the siblings to love the newborn unconditionally. Most, if not all, parents fall in love with their baby long before its birth. In many cases parents begin to pray for their child even before conception. See 1 Samuel 1:8-20 for an example of this kind of love from Hannah. She prayed for a child before he was even conceived in her womb. God granted her wishes and in due time Samuel was born. Scripture clearly shows that Hannah loved Samuel with all of her heart having longed for his birth long before he was born.

However, a newborn baby must learn how to love. At birth a baby has its entire focus on personal comfort. It cries out for food, warmth, diaper changes, and the comforting caresses of his loving parents. Of course, as the baby develops, this rapidly changes. Before long the child is filled with love for his family. Love is from God and it is a joy to see His people learning to love each other just like the Lord commanded.

LOVE PROVES WE ARE BORN OF GOD: Loving one another provides evidence that we are born of God. The failure by children of God to love their fellow man proves they have not been born of God. Or, perhaps it shows they have died spiritually.

LOVE DEMONSTRATES KNOWLEDGE OF GOD: Obviously we cannot know God if we have not poured over the Scriptures and learned of Him. This is a necessary journey for every believer. We can also observe God's creation as a means of getting to know God (Psa. 19:1-2). Another vital way to know God more intimately is to know Jesus. The Lord asked Philip, "How can you say, Show us the Father? Do you not believe that I am in the Father and the Father is in me?" (John 14:9-10).

As we gain more knowledge we learn to know God more intimately. As children of God we have an awesome opportunity to show the world what God's love looks like. Since love comes from God, our love for others should give unbelievers more motivation to learn about the Lord. The more we learn more about God the more our love for others will increase.

GOD IS LOVE: Finally, in verse 8, we learn that God is love. We have already discussed many of the attributes of love. This verse presents a truth that is of supreme importance. It is not that God loves, even though He does. This Scripture tells us that God is love. Love is the very essence of God. Our Heavenly Father didn't have to learn to love because He is love. It can never be said of human beings that we are love. The best we can hope for is to learn how to love. When we fail to love it proves to the world that we do not know God, "because God is love."

GOD'S LOVE REVEALED

> In this the love of God was made manifest among us, that God sent his only Son into the world, so that we might live through him. In this is love, not that we have loved God but that he loved us and sent his Son to be the propitiation for our sins. Beloved, if God so loved us, we also ought to love one another. No one has ever seen God; if we love one another, God abides in us and his love is perfected in us. By this we know that we abide in him and he in us, because he has given us of his Spirit. And we have seen and testify that the Father has sent his Son to be the Savior of the world. Whoever confesses that Jesus is the Son of God, God abides in him, and he in God.
>
> 1 John 4:9-15

God sent His Son into the world as a manifestation of His love for all mankind. The meaning of the Greek word "manifest" is: "to make openly known." Therefore, we learn that God made His love openly known to us by sending His only Son Jesus to this earth. By God's love and Jesus' loving sacrifice we were given the opportunity to live through Him. Jesus said, "I am the life" (John 14:6), demonstrating that He is the giver of life to all those who believe in Him.

NOT THAT WE LOVED GOD: From 1 John 4:10 we learn that it is not that we loved God but that God loved us. How much did He love us? The Father loved us enough to send His only Son to be the propitiation for our sins. You will remember from our discussion of 1 John 2:2 that propitiation means, "concilliation, expiation." It is described by some teachers as a covering. Therefore, when we obey the Gospel of Christ God does not see our sins at all. He only sees the blood of Jesus. It was God's love that motivated Him to make it possible for us to have our sins forgiven. It is not that we loved God but that He loved us. The more one thinks about this truth, the more he will love both the Father and the Son.

GOD'S LOVE IS PERFECTED IN US: "Beloved, if God so loved us, we also ought to love one another, No one has ever seen God; if we love one another, God abides in us and his love is perfected in us" (1 John 4:11-12). This is the last time John used the word "beloved" in 1 John. (See 1 John 2:7; 3:2, 21; 4:1, 7, 11 to observe all six instances.) The apostle now gives us a strong reason for loving one another. That motive is: we love one another because God loves us. Unfortunately, that fact that no man has seen God makes it more difficult for some people to love Him. However, when we do love Him with all our being (Matt. 22:24-39), we provide evidence to others that God abides in us.

If we do not accomplish the commandment to love one another we make God's love incomplete. It can be likened unto unrequited love. Consider a mother with a rebellious son. She loves her son and provides for him. She gives him shelter, food and her full-blown love. If, in spite of her many demonstrations of love, her son despises her, then her love is not perfected. That is true because he fails to love her back. One-way love is never perfect. When we do not love one another we cause the love of God to be incomplete. Perfect love requires that we love one another and that we love God. Only then will God's love be made perfect.

WE ABIDE IN HIM AND HE IN US: "By this we know that we abide in him and he in us, because he has given us of his Spirit. And we have seen and testify that the Father has sent his Son to be the Savior of the world. Whoever confesses that Jesus is the Son of God, God abides in him, and he in God" (1 John 4:13-15). These verses present four important truths in regard to our relationship with God.

1. We abide in Him. This is not new information. John has been telling us this truth over and over again. Evidently it was important to the Spirit to emphasize the word "abide" often.
2. We have been given His Spirit. Again, even though we have heard this truth before isn't it comforting to be reminded once again that the Holy Spirit abides in us? Having the Spirit is evidence that we abide in God.
3. God sent His son. This verse gives us inspired testimony that the Father sent His Son to be the Savior of the world. 1 John 4:13-14. "There is salvation in no one else, for there is no other name under heaven given among men by which we must be saved," Acts 4:12. This verse powerfully refutes the false teaching of the antichrists who were undermining the faith of the brethren to whom John wrote. They claimed Jesus was not the Son of God, 1 John 2:22.
4. Confession proves one abides in Jesus. "Whoever confesses that Jesus is the Son of God abides in Him and He in God". The day after Jesus fed the 5,000 the crowd deserted Him because He told them He was the bread of life. He asked His apostles if they would also leave Him. Peter responded for the group by saying, "Lord, to whom shall we go? You have the words of eternal life and we have believed and have come to know, that you are the Holy One of God," John 6:68-69. We, too, must continually

> confess our belief that the Father sent His Son to be our Savior. This is not just a formula to be said when a person becomes a believer. We should be making a daily confession of our faith in Jesus. By doing so we are able to prove we abide in Him by our words and our deeds.

Thank you Lord for providing us with the blessing of abiding in You and You in us. Thank you, God, for loving us enough to send your Son to save us from our sins. We are truly grateful!

BENEFITS OF GOD'S LOVE

> So we have come to know and to believe the love that God has for us. God is love, and whoever abides in love abides in God, and God abides in him. By this is love perfected with us, so that we may have confidence for the day of judgment, because as he is so also are we in this world. There is no fear in love, but perfect love casts out fear. For fear has to do with punishment, and whoever fears has not been perfected in love.
>
> 1 John 4:16-18

Much of the information given in these three verses repeats doctrines John has already mentioned. However, it is always good for us to hear important biblical truths from God's word over and over again. Repetition helps us to firmly plant biblical truth into our minds. Therefore we do not apologize for discussing these verses even though they contain ideas that have already been stated in earlier verses. After all, the Holy Spirit inspired John to write as he did. That surely tells us that we need to hear that message again!

WE KNOW GOD LOVES US (1 John 4:16): This fact is known through faith. We know the importance of faith and we know its source. "So faith comes from hearing and hearing through the word of Christ" (Rom. 10:17). How comforting is this knowledge to you? It certainly gives me reason to be thankful. God loves me, this I know, because the Bible tells me so!

TO ABIDE IN LOVE IS TO ABIDE IN GOD (1 John 4:16): The way we abide in Him is through our knowledge and belief (faith). The way He abides in us is through knowledge of His word and by the indwelling of the Holy Spirit. It is by the knowledge of God's love we know that we abide in God. In 1 John 4:15 we learned that we also abide in Jesus.

HIS LOVE IS PERFECTED IN US (1 John 4:17): We have already discussed the fact that God's love is not made perfect unless we love Him and His children. Perfect love flows back and forth between God and those who believe. Love also flows back and forth between us and our brothers and sisters in Christ. We must make every effort to achieve the kind of love that makes God's love perfect. To be perfect is to be mature or complete.

LOVE GIVES US CONFIDENCE (1 John 4:17-1): Godly love gives us confidence on the Judgment Day. Fear demonstrates immature love. If you fear the coming of that great day your love is not perfect. We need to grow in love because perfect love casts out fear of punishment. Those fearful of the Day of Judgment are immature in their love. Thank you God for providing us with your perfect love, a love that casts out fear of the Judgment Day.

LOVE YOUR BROTHER – PERIOD!

> We love because he first loved us. If anyone says, "I love God," and hates his brother, he is a liar; for he who does not love his brother whom he has seen cannot love God whom he has not seen. And this commandment we have from him: whoever loves God must also love his brother.
>
> 1 John 4:19-21

John wrote, "We love because he first loved us." Human beings can only love because God showed us the way. We demonstrate the kind of love that came from God when we love our brother. Since God loved us before we loved Him surely we can learn to love our brothers even when they do not love us back.

The person who claims to love God while he hates his brother is a liar. That is very strong language! Scripture clearly states, if we do not love our brother whom we *have seen* we *cannot love God* whom we *have not seen*. Doesn't that make sense? Which is easier? To love someone you have seen or to love someone you have never seen? Loving our brother is a commandment from God. "This commandment we have from him: whoever loves God must also love his brother." Since we know that God does not command us to do the impossible, we know for certain we can learn to love our brothers. Let's get busy doing it.

Heavenly Father, please grant us the ability to love you with all our being and to love our brothers as ourselves. We pray that our love will be the kind of love that makes your love perfect and the kind of love that will cast out all fear of the Judgment Day. We pray that our love will be so much like Yours that it will prove to others that we really do love You!

DISCUSSION QUESTIONS:

1. Discuss what you learned about love from 1 John 4:7-8.
2. Discuss the three main headings listed for 1 John 4:9-15.
3. What steps can you take to learn to love those brethren who are somewhat difficult to love?
4. Think about how difficult it is for you to love sinners? What steps can you take to improve your ability to love sinners?
5. Discuss the four ideas taken from 1 John 4:13-15. What do they say about our relationship with God?

CHAPTER TEN

KNOWLEDGE PROVIDES CONFIDENCE

1 JOHN 5:1-21

LOVE AND OBEDIENCE

> Everyone who believes that Jesus is the Christ has been born of God, and everyone who loves the Father loves whoever has been born of him. By this we know that we love the children of God, when we love God and obey his commandments.
>
> 1 John 5:1-2

BEING BORN OF HIM

John has been teaching multiple aspects of love throughout this epistle. His marvelous discussions on love conclude in 1 John 5:5. Love is an area of life where we should continue to grow until the very last day of our life. Even though we have already learned multiple aspects of godlike love there is still one more discussion we need to consider. That is the relationship between our love for God and the keeping of His commandments.

In reaching this final lesson John will repeat some important truths he has already taught us. The inspired writers of the Bible had no problem repeating important lessons and themes. The apostle Peter repeated himself in 2 Peter 1:12; 3:1-2 without any apology whatsoever. The human mind is such that we need reminders. Otherwise we tend to forget.

In verse 1, we were reminded that our belief (faith) that Jesus is the Christ prompted us to be born again. This is in stark contrast to the teaching of the antichrists who denied the Deity of Jesus (1 John 2:22). Jesus spoke to Nicodemus about the new birth in John 3:1-8. "Truly, truly I say to you, unless one is born of water and the Spirit, he cannot enter the kingdom of God" (John 3:5). Later on, Paul taught we are baptized in the likeness of the death, burial, and resurrection of Christ (Rom. 6:1-7). We come up out the water to "walk in newness of life" (Rom. 6:4). It is when we come up out of the waters of baptism that we begin our new life. The passage in Romans 6 makes it is easy to see that the new birth occurs when we are baptized into Christ.

The book of Acts shows that people were brought to faith when they heard the gospel. After believing the good news of Christ they repented and were immersed in water (baptized) to wash away their sins (Acts 22:16). It is only when we fulfill all of the requirements put forth in the Gospel of Christ that we receive the promise of salvation. Faith in Jesus brings us to obedience and obedience brings about our new birth. "So you also must consider yourselves dead to sin and alive to God in Christ Jesus" (Rom. 6:7). Baptized believers become slaves of righteousness rather than slaves of sin (Rom. 6:17-18). Believers are born again and then they begin to live a new life in service to the Master.

In 1 John 5:1-2 we learn that those who believe that Jesus is the Christ have been born of God. We also learn, as believers, we truly love God as well as everyone who has been born of Him. Over and over again the apostle John has revealed to us the importance of brotherly love. However, in these verses he connects brotherly love with obedience. "By this we know that we love the children of God, when we love God and obey his commandments." Our love for each other proves that we love God. Our love for God causes us to obey his commandments. How important is that?

VICTORY OVER THE WORLD

> For this is the love of God, that we keep his commandments. And his commandments are not burdensome. For everyone who has been born of God overcomes the world. And this is the victory that has overcome the world—our faith. Who is it that overcomes the world except the one who believes that Jesus is the Son of God?
>
> 1 John 5:3-5

Verse three teaches us if we love God we will keep His commandments. In 1 John 4:19-21 we learned it is impossible to love the Father if we hate our brother. However, our claim to be a child of God is also validated when we keep His commandments. Believers have been born of God. Our faith gives us the victory over the world. Only those who believe that Jesus is the Son of God will experience this victory.

KEEPING THE COMMANDMENTS

Far too many people consider keeping the commandments of God to be a huge burden even though John wrote, "His commandments are not burdensome". Others misunderstand the grace of God and think there are no longer any commandments for us to keep. The apostle John disagreed with that doctrine when he said, "For this is the love of God, that we keep his commandments."

Have you ever considered that love for God requires keeping His commandments? To disobey is the sin of rebellion. Believers should not think God's commandments to be burdensome. The Greek word "burdensome" means, "heavy, oppressive, hard to be borne, weighty". Some people find no joy in Sunday worship. Others consider loving one another to be a burden that is beyond their ability to accomplish. Our *great love for God* should prompt us to keep His commandments and to do so with joy. However, there is another component to consider before we leave this topic and that is our faith.

FAITH IS THE VICTORY!

Faith is the victory that overcomes the world. The world, as mentioned here, has the same meaning we discussed in 1 John 2:15-17. It speaks of the sinful things of this world. Faith provides the key for the child of God to overcome worldly passions. The Greek word "overcome" means: "to be victorious, come off victor, conquer." Faith that leads to obedience gives us the victory. Increase your faith and you increase your ability to keep the commandments of the Lord. "Who is it that overcomes the world except the one who believes that Jesus is the Son of God?" (1 John 5:5). It is only those who possess this kind of faith that will be successful. "Thanks be to God, who gives us the victory through our Lord Jesus Christ" (1 Cor. 15:57).

THE THREE WITNESSES – 1 JOHN 5:6-8

Some English translations of the Bible add words to 1 John 5:6-8 that are unauthorized. You can research this problem by reading from Greek scholars who address the issue. A comparison of the King James Version and the English Standard Version will help identify the unauthorized words that are found in the King James Version. They are in bold print for easy identification. Priscillian, a Spanish heretic, placed the words into his 1 John manuscript. He died in A.D. 395. Unfortunately, the men who translated the King James Version in 1611 included Priscillian's additions to their English translation. The ESV provides a preferred translation of 1 John 5:6-8. There are also other English translations that leave the unauthorized words out of their translation of the Bible.

> This is he who came by water and blood—Jesus Christ; not by the water only but by the water and the blood. And the Spirit is the one who testifies, because the Spirit is the truth. For there are three that testify: the Spirit and the water and the blood; and these three agree.
>
> 1 John 5:6–8 (ESV)

> This is he that came by water and blood, even Jesus Christ; not by water only, but by water and blood. And it is the Spirit that beareth witness, because the Spirit is truth. For there are three that bear record **in heaven, the Father, the Word, and the Holy Ghost: and these three are one. And there are three that bear witness in earth,** the spirit, and the water, and the blood: and these three agree in one.
>
> 1 John 5:6–8 (KJV)

The first two witnesses are "water" and "blood." "This is he who came by water" is a very difficult passage to understand. According to many commentators it is one of the most difficult verses in the entire New Testament. J. W. Roberts, author of the *Sweet Commentary on the Epistles of John*, presents the following major interpretations: "(1) the water and blood which came from Jesus' side when pierced in death, John 19:34, an interpretation offered by Augustine, Speaker's Commentary, an F. W. Farrar; (2) the ordinances of baptism and the Lord's supper (Calvin and Luther); (3) purification and redemption; and (4) the water of Jesus' baptism and the blood shed in his death" (*The Letters of John*, J. W. Roberts, page 130). The fourth explanation makes the most sense to me. WATER: Jesus was baptized in water and then His ministry began. BLOOD: The Lord shed His blood on the cross providing forgiveness for our sins. The work God gave Him to do on earth began after his baptism and ended with His crucifixion and ascension. Speaking of the water and blood was John's way of speaking of the entire ministry of Jesus on earth. This is the most plausible explanation of the first two witnesses.

The third witness is the Holy Spirit who is called the Spirit of truth (John 15:26). Truth is also descriptive of God and Jesus. It is easy to see that the Godhead (God the Father, God the Son and God the Holy Spirit) is truth. No one could possibly find a more reliable witness than the Holy Spirit. All three statements (blood, water, and Spirit) are one, meaning they are in total agreement with each other. Therefore the Spirit, the water, and the blood unite in agreement with John's testimony about Jesus Christ.

RELIABILITY OF THE WITNESSES

> If we receive the testimony of men, the testimony of God is greater, for this is the testimony of God that he has borne concerning his Son. Whoever believes in the Son of God has the testimony in himself. Whoever does not believe God has made him a liar, because he has not believed in the testimony that God has borne concerning his Son. And this is the testimony, that God gave us eternal life, and this life is in his Son. Whoever has the Son has life; whoever does not have the Son of God does not have life.
>
> 1 John 5:9-12

We will now take a look at the reliability of the witnesses. In the Old Testament we learn that charges could not be made against anyone without the testimony of two or three witnesses, Deuteronomy 19:15. A court of law always seeks testimony from eyewitnesses who have firsthand knowledge of the case. If we accept the witness of fleshly men (and we do) then we must, of necessity, accept the testimony of God. Jehovah God Himself bore witness that Jesus *is* His Son. We can trust that testimony without any reservation.

GOD'S TESTIMONY

What was the testimony God presented to us? It is two-fold. First, He testified that Jesus is His Son (1 John 5:9). This destroys the arguments of the antichrists. Secondly, He testified that He gave us eternal life in His Son (1 John 5:11). The arguments of the antichrists have now been completely invalidated. Jesus is the Son of God and through Him we have the opportunity to obtain eternal life. After all, life is in the Son. Therefore, He can give life to His followers. This testimony comes from the Spirit of truth and that gives us two witnesses. Those who believe in the Son of God are also witnesses (1 John 5:10). Thus we have God, the Spirit, and the believers all giving the same testimony concerning Jesus Christ. What is their testimony? It is that Jesus is God's Son.

The gnostic claims make God a liar (1 John 5:9). However, the Bible clearly states that "it is impossible for God to lie" (Heb. 6:18). God, who cannot lie, gives testimony that (1) Jesus is His Son. (2) Eternal life is in His Son. There is no spiritual life for those who do not have the Son.

FINAL INSTRUCTIONS

> I write these things to you who believe in the name of the Son of God that you may know that you have eternal life.
>
> 1 John 5:13

It is a sad thing when believers doubt their salvation. The believer should have absolute confidence that heaven will be his eternal home. He should have complete assurance that he is saved and that he has eternal life (1 John 5:13). This verse contains the last of five purpose statements John gave for writing this epistle. John wrote so "you may know that you have eternal life" (1 John 5:13). If you wish, you can review John's purpose statements by looking in Chapter One of this commentary.

John wrote in order to encourage us about our heavenly home and to remove any doubts we might have about receiving our reward. John provided additional reassurance for us when he wrote, "Be faithful until death and I will give you the crown of life" (Rev. 2:10). The text does not say you will have eternal life it says, "you have eternal life." I find that to be very comforting news. How about you?

CONFIDENCE IN PRAYER

> And this is the confidence that we have toward him, that if we ask anything according to his will he hears us. And if we know that he hears us in whatever we ask, we know that we have the requests that we have asked of him.
>
> 1 John 5:14-15

Children of God have the privilege of talking to the Creator of heaven and earth anytime night or day. God's ear is always open to us unless we are guilty of committing habitual sins. If we ignore our sins we are no longer walking in the light and He will not hear our prayers. Why? Because "your iniquities have made a separation between you and your God, and your sins have hidden his face from you so that he does not hear" (Isa. 59:2). However, the faithful have confidence that He not only hears them but that they will receive a positive answer to the things they ask of God. That is definitely true when they ask according to His will. How encouraging is that?

Someone might counter, "I asked God for many things I did not receive. He has not answered all of my prayers." For the faithful child of God this statement is *not true*. The Lord our God answers every request we make of Him. God answers our prayers but He does not always answer with "yes." We are often like children and, as such, we sometimes ask for things that are not in our best interest. Those requests are answered "no." Make no mistake about it, even if we don't like the answer, "no" is still an answer. A case could be made that such prayers are not according to His will.

Here are some ways our prayers are answered. (1) Yes. This is the answer to every request we make that is according to His will. (2) No. This is God's answer to requests that are not according to His will. (3) Later. Sometimes the Lord defers a positive answer until later. That is because God, in His wisdom, knows it is not the right time for us to receive our request. (4) Persistent prayer. There are other times when a negative response is turned into a "yes" due to our persistence. Read the parable of the persistent widow in Luke 18:1-8 to learn the value of persistence. The unrighteous judge, a figure representing God, turned the woman down many times but her persistence in asking changed his mind. The woman is a figure of us when we pray. The case is made in this parable that God will sometimes change His mind and give us our requests due to our persistence. Sometimes God's "no" can be turned into "yes". In each case God did answer the prayers of His righteous ones. He did so in a way that was the best for His children.

We learn from Paul that sometimes we just do not know how to pray like we should. That is why the Holy Spirit, who dwells in us, intercedes for us when we do not know what to say. The Spirit takes those things we don't know how to say to God on our behalf (Rom. 8:26-28). From this passage we also learn that God always works things out for our good. Our God is a gracious God and He wants to bless His children.

PRAYER AND SIN

> If anyone sees his brother committing a sin not leading to death, he shall ask, and God will give him life – to those who commit sins that do not lead to death. There is sin that leads to death; I do not say that one should pray for that. All wrongdoing is sin, but there is a sin that does not lead to death.
>
> 1 John 5:16-17

PRAYING FOR EACH OTHER

Isn't it wonderful to know that we can pray for others and, in like manner, they can pray for us? Thank you Lord for providing us with yet another avenue to receive help when we sin. While no human has the power to remove the sins of another person, we can certainly go to God on their behalf. We can pray that the sinner will realize the error of his ways and that he will do whatever he needs to do in order to get right with God. Surely God can use us in other ways in addition to our prayers to encourage a sinner to turn back to a righteousness lifestyle.

A SIN NOT UNTO DEATH

What is a sin that is *not unto death*? Many find this to be a difficult passage. We know for sure that God does not forgive other people because of any power we have to forgive sin. Forgiveness of sin is God's domain. The sin not unto death is a sin that is not being committed over and over again (habitually). It speaks of the failure of someone who slips and falls into sin. This person did not intend to do wrong but he did. We learned in 1 John 1:8 that no one can claim he has no sins in the present time. This is a person for whom we can pray because he still has a tender heart and can be brought to repentance. It is inferred that we can also speak with the brother who committed a sin.

When Simon sinned in Acts 8, Peter condemned him. Simon was frightened and touched by the severity of his error and he asked Peter to pray for him (Acts 8:19-24). This is a good example of talking to an erring brother and then praying for him. A person like Simon, when made aware of his error, will repent and ask God for forgiveness. In addition, he will cease to commit his sin whatever it might be. When he repents he will be given life because he has made himself right with God. Such a sin is not a sin unto death.

A SIN UNTO DEATH

There is "a sin that leads to death". This is the person who is guilty of committing the same sin(s) over and over again. This person continues in their sinful ways with no intention of repentance. The people of Judah were like that in the days of Jeremiah. They habitually sinned with no intention of changing their ways. Consequently, God told Jeremiah "Do not pray for this people, or lift up a cry or prayer for them, and do not intercede with me for I will not hear you" (Jer. 7:16). The command not to pray for the habitual sinner is repeated in Jeremiah 14:12 when God clearly condemned Judah for her sins. "I will not accept them. But I will consume them by the sword, by famine, and by pestilence." Do not think that God will bless you if you commit the same sins habitually with no remorse nor intention to repent. We are reminded of our sin problem in 1 John 5:16. "There is sin that leads to death; I do not say that one should pray for that." Pray that you will never be guilty of a sin like that. Such a sin could cause you to be lost. For a review on sin, read the discussion of 1 John 3:4-10 found in Chapter Six of this commentary.

GODLY PROTECTION

> We know that everyone who has been born of God does not keep on sinning, but he who was born of God protects him, and the evil one does not touch him. We know that we are from God, and the whole world lies in the power of the evil one. And we know that the Son of God has come and has given us understanding, so that we may know him who is true; and we are in him who is true, in his Son Jesus Christ. He is the true God and eternal life.
>
> 1 John 5:18-20

People who have been born of God refuse to keep doing sinful things. As soon as this person is aware of sin in his life he acknowledges his wrongdoing before God. He then goes back to walking in the light as He is in the light (1 John 1:7). His success is rooted in the fact that he is born of God and thereby he receives Divine protection (1 John 5:18). It is comforting to know that the children of God receive God's help and are shielded from the power of the evil one. When we are walking in the light and when we acknowledge our sins we become untouchable. "God protects us and the evil one does not touch him." I love the contrast given in 5:19. We (believers) are from God. They (unbelievers) are under the power of the evil one. "They" refers to the sinful world.

In 1 John 5:20 we learn several important truths. (1) We learn that the Son of God has come. (2) He gave us understanding so that we could know Him who is true. Some say this speaks of knowing God while others say it speaks of Jesus. In the context of the verse it seems more logical to understand it is speaking of Jesus. (3) We are in Him who is true. This certainly speaks of Jesus. (4) Jesus is the true God and eternal life. Read John 1:1-4 for confirmation that Jesus is God. In Isaiah 9:6 Jesus is called "Everlasting Father". Jesus was also named Immanuel, meaning "God with us" (Matt. 1:23).

The Gnostics denied that Jesus was the Son of God (Divine). They would never call Jesus God. However, "We are in him who is true, in his Son Jesus Christ. He is the true God and eternal life." This passage makes a powerful statement that completely destroys the false doctrine being taught by the antichrists. Understanding who Jesus is will lead us to eternal life (1 John 5:20).

BEWARE OF IDOLATRY!

> Little children, keep yourselves from idols.
>
> 1 John 5:21

Finally, we are commanded to keep away from idols. What is an idol? It is a god made with human hands. We learn how useless idols are when we read Psalm

115. We know how the Nations in and around Israel were an idolatrous people who worshipped graven images. Even the Nation of Israel became guilty of worshipping pagan idols. Isaiah 44:9-20 demonstrates the folly of idol worship. With half the tree he prepares his food and with the other half he prays, "Deliver me, for you are my god!" Such a person "feeds on ashes; a deluded heart has led him astray" (Isa. 44:20).

However, it is incorrect to believe that only those who fall down before graven images are guilty of idolatry. Our idols could be gods made with human hands, or it could be our husband, our wife, or our children. It could be greed or covetousness. "Put to death . . . covetousness which is idolatry," (Col. 3:5). *Anything* we put in the place that belongs to Jehovah God becomes our idol. Even our pleasurable pastimes can become our gods. Some people even make themselves their god. Be diligent to keep yourselves from idols of any kind because such actions will bring the wrath of the Lord God upon you.

God commanded Israel, "You shall have no other gods before me" (Exod. 20:3). The commandment God gave to Israel is still valid. Jehovah is still not pleased when we worship manmade idols. Take John's advice "keep yourselves from idols."

DISCUSSION QUESTIONS:

1. Discuss how we know we love the children of God from 1 John 5:1-2.
2. Discuss the process of loving God and being born of Him (1 John 5:1).
3. What is the victory that overcomes the world from 1 John 5:3-5?
4. Discuss 1 John 5:6-8 and the three witnesses.
5. Who are the reliable witnesses who gave testimony in 1 John 5:9-12?
6. How can we have assurance of eternal life (1 John 5:13)?
7. Discuss prayer for sinners, including sins not unto death and sins unto

death from 1 John 5:16-17.

8. How would you define idolatry in today's world? Discuss some idolatrous practices found in today's world.

CHAPTER ELEVEN

WALKING IN THE TRUTH

2 JOHN

INTRODUCTION AND OUTLINE

The church that received this epistle was being troubled by antichrists and they did not seem to know what to do about it. The apostle John became God's man to step up and address the situation. Every congregation needs a faithful person with Bible knowledge to help them address doctrinal problems when they arise. If the situation is ignored the church will have turmoil over those differences in doctrine and they could be in danger of apostasy. This short epistle contains only thirteen verses but they are power packed with extremely important lessons we need to learn.

Our theme is: Walking In The Truth. Knowledge of the truth is the only weapon we have against false doctrine. Believers in every age must know enough to refute any false teaching that might come their way. Our ability to stand is "because of the truth that abides in us and will be with us forever" (2 John 1:2).

John, the son of Zebedee, wrote this epistle on one sheet of papyrus paper. The same is true of the following books: Philemon, 3 John, and Jude. Papyrus is made from the Papyrus reed, a plant common to Egypt. Later in history, during the fifth century A.D., animal skins called vellum became the favored writing material.

IMPORTANT WORDS

This short epistle contains four words that are repeated several times. This demonstrates how import they are. We should consider them carefully.

1. TRUTH: Used 5 times: Twice in verse 1, once in verses 2, 3, 4.
2. LOVE: Used 4 times: once in verses 1, 3, 5, 6.
3. COMMANDMENT: Used 4 times: Once verses 4-5 and twice in verse 6.
4. DOCTRINE (teaching): Used 3 times: Twice in verse 9 and once in verse 10.

THE VALUE OF THE EPISTLE

Second John provides us with valuable information on the proper way to deal with brethren who teach false doctrines. This epistle calls them deceivers and antichrists (against Christ). The brethren are told not to have fellowship with those false teachers. We must be constantly on guard in order to ensure we are walking in the truth of God's word.

A BRIEF OUTLINE OF SECOND JOHN

1. Greetings From The Elder (1:1-3)
   a. To the "elect lady" (1:1-2).
   b. Greeting (1:3)
2. Divine Orders to Obey (1:4-11)
   a. To love (1:4-5)
   b. To obedience (1:6)

c. To be alert to dangers (1:7-8).

d. To refusal of error (1:9-11

3. Final Greetings (1:12-13)

a. Hope for a future visit (1:12)

b. Greetings from your elect sister (1:13)

GREETINGS FROM THE ELDER

> The elder to the elect lady and her children, whom I love in truth, and not only I, but also all who know the truth, because of the truth that abides in us and will be with us forever: Grace, mercy, and peace will be with us, from God the Father and from Jesus Christ the Father's Son, in truth and love.
>
> 2 John 1:1-3

THE ELDER

Conservative scholars name John, the son of Zebedee as the author of this epistle. John merely identifies himself as the "elder." What does he mean by the term? Was he speaking of himself as a church official who held the office of "elder"? Of course, that is possible. We know for certain that the apostle Peter served as both an apostle and an elder (1 Pet. 5:1-5). There are others who suggest he is speaking as a mature Christian speaking to those who were children in the faith. It is impossible to be dogmatic about the meaning. However, it seems reasonable to me to believe this last explanation to be correct. That is, John was an elder (mature) in the faith having been with Jesus from the very beginning. The recipients of the letter were called children (immature), meaning they were relatively new in the faith. It is possible that John was in some way involved in their conversion or their follow-up training in the faith.

THE ELECT LADY

The reason John addressed this epistle to the "elect lady" is not all that clear. Scholars offer three explanations of the term. You will have to decide for yourself which explanation to accept.

AN UNIDENTIFIED WOMAN: Some say the term is used to describe an unidentified woman to whom John wrote. If this is true, John also references her sister and her children in verse 13.

ELECT LADY: Other scholars believe John wrote to a faithful woman in the church and to her children. Here is the explanation. John addresses her as "eklekte kuria." The Greek word "eklekte" means, "elect, chosen." Thayer, defines the word to mean "the best of its kind, or class, excellent, preeminent: applied to an individual." Kuria in the Greek, means "Lady. It is also a proper name, 'Kuria.' Used as an honorable title of address." Some scholars claim John was addressing a woman who was addressed by the title "Elect lady." If Kuria is her name the greeting would become "Elect Kuria" (lady) an outstanding Christian to whom John wrote.

THE CHURCH: Other scholars claim the phrase is John's way of identifying the church to which he wrote. They explain that "Elect Lady" is a phrase meaning the church as a whole. The phrase "her children" is used to indicate all of the individual members of the congregation. This explanation makes the most sense to me.

When you consider the fact that the Roman persecution against the church was at an all-time high when John wrote it makes sense that he would try to protect the identity of the people who received this epistle. It was prudent for him to be vague in regards to the people and their location. It was a means of protecting the church against Roman persecution.

You will have to decide for yourself which explanation makes more sense to you. Personally, I agree with the explanation that says the lady is the church and her children are the individual members of the congregation. Thus the epistle was addressed to everyone in the congregation.

TRUTH AND LOVE

Before addressing the problems the antichrists brought to the church John expressed his genuine love for this group of believers. He lets them know the brethren where John lived loved them too. It is godly for us to love all of God's people.

GREETINGS

Verse 3 invokes three wonderful blessings God gives to His people. The blessings are: Grace, Mercy, and Peace. The source of these blessings is God the Father, and Jesus Christ. The Holy Spirit moved John to use the phrase "Jesus Christ the Father's Son" to counter the teachings of the antichrists who claimed that Jesus was not the Son of God and that He was not God made flesh (1 John 2:22, 2 John 1:7).

Grace (*charis*) is defined as "a free gift, unmerited favor." Grace is something we do not deserve to receive but is a blessing freely given by God to believers. Paul wrote about grace in Ephesians 2:1-10. He explains how we are saved by grace and not by works. However verse 10 informs us that we were created to do good works. This sounds contradictory but it is not. We work out of gratitude for all God has done for us, not in order to earn our salvation. We work because we love God and have a strong desire to serve Him.

Mercy (*eleos*) is defined as, "a feeling of sympathy with misery, active compassion, the desire of relieving the miserable, hence; benefits bestowed upon the miserable." Aren't you thrilled to know that our God is a God of mercy! According to Jesus, we only receive mercy from God when we show mercy to others (Matt. 5:7). The Lord told a parable about a man who was forgiven a huge debt by a King but refused to have mercy on a man who owed him only a small debt. The forgiving King condemned the man for failing to show the same kind of mercy to the poor man that he himself had received. We need to know that God only gives mercy to those who show mercy (Matt. 18:21-35). I like the idea that mercy includes a strong desire to relieve the misery of others.

Peace (*eirene*) is defined as "peace or rest in contrast to strife." Jesus promised to give us His peace (John 14:27). It should not surprise us that the Lord's peace is different from the peace offered by the world. The world usually defines peace as the cessation of conflict. The Prince of Peace gives us a different kind of peace. It is "the peace of God, which surpasses understanding" (Phil. 4:7). Paul also wrote that without peace and holiness no man will see God (Heb. 12:14). Seek Jesus' peace. He has made it available to us. One of my teachers told me years ago that the peace Jesus gives doesn't depend upon our circumstances. He taught:

1. We will have peace when we have the right relationship between God and ourselves.
2. We will have peace when we have the right relationship between our fellow man and ourselves.
3. We will have peace when we are at peace with ourselves.

Never forget that grace, mercy, and peace come from God the Father and from Jesus Christ His Son. John describes Christians as a people who love the truth of God's word. We also love those who know the truth, and we are a people in whom the truth abides forever (2 John 1:1-2). Everyone who abides in truth and love will enjoy these blessings.

TO LOVE

> I rejoiced greatly to find some of your children walking in the truth, just as we were commanded by the Father. And now I ask you, dear lady—not as though I were writing you a new commandment, but the one we have had from the beginning—that we love one another.
>
> 2 John 1:4-5

Perhaps some of the members of the church went to visit John in order to discuss the false teaching of the antichrists. John called them "children walking in the truth." The apostle commended them for their walk. To have such a walk is not an option for the child of God. It is a requirement. It is interesting to find so many passages in the New Testament that speak of walking. Why not look up the word "walk" in a New Testament concordance and study the context of every verse containing the word. You will find it to be a very enlightening study. Walking in the truth is not an option for children of God.

The reference to "dear lady" in verse 5 refers to the entire congregation. The church was told to love one another just as they were told from the beginning. As you know, loving one another is the second greatest commandment. Read the discussion on 1 John 2:7-9 found in Chapter Seven of this commentary for a review on "loving one another."

TO OBEDIENCE

> And this is love, that we walk according to his commandments; this is the commandment, just as you have heard from the beginning, so that you should walk in it.
>
> 2 John 1:6

Verse 6 is actually the conclusion to verses 4-5. The verse shows us that loving one another provides evidence that we are walking according to the commandments. To walk indicates movement towards an objective, which is to walk according to His commandments. Love and obedience are not the same things. However, love provides us with the motivation to be obedient. Why do we love each other? We do so because the God who is love commanded us to do so. Why do we obey? We obey because we love God (1 John 5:1-5). The beginning refers to the beginning of the church as recorded in Acts chapters one and two. Something new began on the day of Pentecost. From that day forward believers were taught to abide in the apostle's doctrine (Acts 2:42). If anyone teaches a doctrine different than that of the Apostles do *not* follow them!

TO BE ALERT TO DANGERS

> For many deceivers have gone out into the world, those who do not confess the coming of Jesus Christ in the flesh. Such a one is the deceiver and the antichrist. Watch yourselves, so that you may not lose what we have worked for, but may win a full reward.
>
> 2 John 1:7-8

We are now alerted that the antichrists were deceivers. We also learn that there are many of them. The word "deceiver" is a word that means "seducing, a religious imposter or teacher of error." This verse speaks of those who did not confess that Jesus Christ came in the flesh. It is difficult to understand how anyone could come to such a conclusion in light of the abundance of biblical teaching on the subject. The following scriptures prove beyond a doubt that Jesus did come in the flesh (Isa. 7:14; 9:6-7; Micah 5:2; Matt. 1:18-23; Luke 2:8-20).

Verse eight gives a stern warning for believers to be watchful lest they lose their reward. Self-examination is a requirement for the children of God. The Apostle Paul used the imagery of training for an athletic event to describe our need to keep our spiritual life under control (1 Cor. 9:24-27). Paul did not want to become guilty of preaching to others while he, himself, was disqualified because of sinful practices. He taught, "Examine yourselves to see whether you are in the faith. Test yourselves. Or do you not realize this about yourselves, that Jesus Christ is in you? –unless indeed you fail to meet the test!" (2 Cor. 13:5).

There are many who believe a person who is truly saved cannot lose his reward. John taught otherwise. We must be careful not to go beyond what is written. It is possible for us not to go far enough and it is also possible for us to go too far. Anyone who denies that Jesus came in the flesh will not win a full reward. That is the reason John gave us such a strong warning. Watch yourselves! There is much at stake!

TO REFUSAL OF ERROR

> Everyone who goes on ahead and does not abide in the teaching of Christ, does not have God. Whoever abides in the teaching has both the Father and the Son. If anyone comes to you and does not bring this teaching, do not receive him into your house or give him any greeting, for whoever greets him takes part in his wicked works.
>
> 2 John 1:9-11

When anyone calling himself a brother brings a doctrine that is different from that which was taught by the Apostles and other inspired writers, we must reject both the teacher and his teaching. However, don't misunderstand. Before fellowship with a brother or sister is severed we must make every effort to restore such a one from the error of his ways. It is only when they persist in their error that we are to follow the instructions given in this passage.

In order to abide in the teaching we must allow the truth to take up a permanent dwelling place in our hearts. We must listen to the advice of Moses who said, "You shall not add to the word that I command you, nor take from it, that you may keep the commandments of the Lord your God that I command you" (Deut. 4:2). Solomon wrote, "Do not add to his words, lest he rebuke you and you be found a liar" (Prov. 30:6). The antichrists had gone too far. How about us? We need to examine our beliefs by the written Word of God. When we abide in the teaching that comes from the Lord, then it can be said of us that we abide in "both the Father and the Son" (2 John 1:9). In the verses under consideration we are receiving advice on the need to be watchful lest we lose our eternal reward.

The instructions John gave on how the church was to deal with the antichrists were twofold. (1) They were not to receive the false teachers into their houses. (2) They were not to give them any greeting. Failure to follow these instructions would make the faithful member just as guilty as the false teachers. The actions the church was to take against the false teachers would sever the bonds of fellowship between the antichrists and the brethren.

The primary purpose of discipline is never to punish the offender but is intended to bring them back to faithful service. The design and purpose of withholding fellowship is to cause those in error to acknowledge their sin. The fervent desire of the faithful is to bring the offenders back to the truth (Jas. 5:19-20). Disciplining a brother in Christ is never a time to rejoice. It is always a time for sadness and for tears!

Remember, if the faithful do not carry out these instructions they become partakers of the sins of the false teachers. What were the "wicked works" of the antichrists? It was their claim that Jesus was not the Son of God and their denial that He came in the flesh.

Isn't it startling to learn that a person doesn't have to believe error to condone it? Granting fellowship to a brother who teaches error or giving him greetings makes you just as guilty of sin as the false teacher himself. These verses teach us the steps we must take when brethren teach false doctrines in the church.

FINAL GREETINGS

> Though I have much to write to you, I would rather not use paper and ink. Instead I hope to come to you and talk face to face, so that our joy may be complete. The children of your elect sister greet you.
>
> 2 John 1:12-13

HOPE FOR A FUTURE VISIT

Finally, John expresses his desire to visit the brethren in person. He confirms his need to say more than what he has written in this epistle. However, John doesn't want to handle the problem strictly by a letter. He wants to visit them personally. Did you notice the mention of "paper and ink"? "Papyrus" is a Greek word for the paper that was made from the papyrus plant.

Notice that the stated intention of the apostle was to visit them in person sometime in the future. He did not want to come for the purpose of scolding or to punish them. He wanted to come in order to talk through their problems face to face. Issues can usually be settled more easily when we sit down together and talk things out. He wanted to visit with them personally so that their mutual joy might be made complete.

GREETING FROM YOUR ELECT SISTER

The epistle closes with greetings from "your elect sister." If we are correct in saying the Elect Lady is a church and that her children are individual members of the congregation then we are correct in saying "your elect sister" refers to members of a sister congregation. It is probably none other than the church at Ephesus. After all, that is where most historians say the apostle John spent his later days.

DISCUSSION QUESTIONS:

1. What is the theme of 2 John?
2. Discuss the four important words found in 2 John.
    - Truth
    - Love
    - Commandment
    - Doctrine

3. What do you think the terms “elect lady”, “your children”, and “your elect sister” mean?
4. Second John 1:4-11 gives us four divine orders to obey. Discuss them.
    - Commandment to love
    - Commandment to obedience
    - To be alert to the dangers
    - To refusal of error
5. How are we to treat false teachers who refuse to give up their error?
6. What is the desired outcome of withholding fellowship from others?

CHAPTER TWELVE

RECEIVE FAITHFUL BRETHREN

3 JOHN

INTRODUCTION AND OUTLINE

The theme of this epistle is "receive faithful brethren." The apostle John and his faithful co-workers were in complete harmony on the topic of assisting traveling evangelists. They were to gladly receive these preachers when they came to town. They also counted it a privilege to supply the financial needs for those who came into their congregation. Their assistance was offered both in word and in deed.

We will meet the elder, who is the apostle John, and Gaius a man who was walking in the truth. Gaius had a mind set to provide for the needs of traveling evangelists who came his way. Towards the end of the epistle we will meet a man named Demetrius, a disciple who was well spoken of by everyone.

However, in the middle of the epistle, John speaks of a trouble-making leader named Diotrephes. He was a demanding self-centered leader who abused the privilege of leadership. Diotrephes refused to welcome visiting evangelists and he also refused to allow the church to supply any of their financial needs. He abused his power by casting out those church members who dared to support the visiting preachers. Therefore, this epistle not only lauds faithful brethren but it also demonstrates how ungodly church leaders can divide and defeat the good work of a congregation.

The apostle wrote his epistle on one sheet of papyrus just as he did 2 John. In the past John had written to Diotrephes but he refused to accept John's letter. Consequently, the apostle planned to make a visit soon so that he could talk to everyone face-to-face. There are times when meeting personally and talking eye-to-eye is the best way to settle a problem. Third John was written in the mid or late 90s A.D. It was a personal letter to Gaius.

OUTLINE OF 3 JOHN: RECEIVE FAITHFUL BRETHREN

1. Faithful Gaius (1:1-8).
2. A warning to Diotrephes (1:9-10).
3. Demetrius is commended (1:11-12).
4. Final greetings (1:13-15).

A BELOVED AND FAITHFUL SERVANT

> The elder to the beloved Gaius, whom I love in truth. Beloved, I pray that all may go well with you and that you may be in good health, as it goes well with your soul. For I rejoiced greatly when the brothers came and testified to your truth, as indeed you are walking in the truth. I have no greater joy than to hear that my children are walking in the truth.
>
> 3 John 1:1-4

Once again the apostle identifies himself by the term "elder." It is the same greeting found in the opening of 2 John. We already stated that it is reasonable to believe that John was speaking of himself as an older person who was speaking to those who were younger in the faith.

There are three men named Gaius in the New Testament. It was evidently a common name in the first century. There was (1) Gaius of Macedonia. He was with Paul during the riot in Ephesus (Acts 19:29). (2) Gaius of Derbe who was one of the delegates chosen to take the collection of money to the poor in Jerusalem (Acts 20:4). (3) Gaius of Corinth was one of the few persons baptized by the hand of the apostle Paul himself (1 Cor. 1:14).

It is impossible for us to know for sure which man named Gaius received the epistle of 3 John. There is a possibility that he is not mentioned anywhere in the New Testament except here in this epistle. We don't even know the location of the church Gaius attended. The lack of knowledge on these details does not change the importance of the message in any way whatsoever. What we do know is that Gaius was a strong Christian who was a joy to the heart of the apostle John. Through this epistle we also learn that churches in the first century had their problems just like churches do in the present day.

The descriptions of Gaius in verses 1-4 are worthy of note. Because Gaius had been cast out of the church for his good Christian service we can assume he was a bit discouraged. Perhaps that is why the apostle used so many encouraging words at the very beginning of 3 John. We should all strive to serve the Lord in the same faithful manner as Gaius. Here are the commendations bestowed upon this faithful Christian worker.

GAIUS WAS BELOVED: Earlier in this commentary we observed that the term "beloved" was used six times in the Epistle of 1 John. It is used an additional 4 times in this short epistle. Take a moment to read all of 3 John in order to identify the times the word "beloved" is used. I cannot think of a closer relationship than to call someone beloved. It is definitely a term of endearment.

GAIUS WAS LOVED: John loved this man in truth. There was nothing phony about their relationship. The apostle was not being insincere in his admiration of Gaius. No doubt they had spent enough time together to become good friends as well as co-workers in the gospel. John loved Gaius in the truth. Isn't it wonderful how the truth binds us together in love?

GAIUS WAS HEALTHY IN BODY AND SOUL: The apostle made a profound statement in this verse! He prayed that Gaius' physical health would match the health of his spirit. This prayer was offered because John recognized the spiritual strength of Gaius. For some people such a prayer would be a curse to their physical wellbeing. Such a prayer would likely cause some people to drop dead on the spot. If our own physical health were suddenly called to match our spiritual health would we gain physical strength or would we need to enter ICU? Food for thought isn't it!

GAIUS WAS COMMENDED FOR HIS WALK: Evidently some faithful members of the congregation made a trip to visit with the apostle John to discuss the problems taking place in their congregation. They wanted John to understand what Diotrephes had done to Gaius and to others who attempted to assist the traveling evangelist who passed their way. These brothers testified to the truth and to the Christian walk of Gaius. His walk caused great joy for the apostle. I know from personal experience the joy faithful disciples bring to an evangelist. As a missionary I planted churches and baptized people into Christ in Asia and in America. It is always wonderful to hear news that some of those you taught are growing in faith and are walking in the truth.

Such news always brings great joy to the hearts of the faithful. John considered Gaius to be one of his spiritual children. The phrase "my children" might infer that Gaius was taught and converted by John himself. At the very least the term indicates that Gaius was under John's care. It always causes a teacher to rejoice when he hears the news of the faithful walk of his "children" in the faith.

GAIUS' FAITHFUL SERVICE

> Beloved, it is a faithful thing you do in all your efforts for these brothers, strangers as they are, who testified to your love be-

> fore the church. You will do well to send them on their journey in a manner worthy of God. For they have gone out for the sake of the name, accepting nothing from the Gentiles. Therefore we ought to support people like these, that we may be fellow workers for the truth.
>
> 3 John 1:5-8

Gaius is now commended for his faithful efforts to assist the strangers (traveling evangelists) who came by the church where he worshipped. These men are called strangers because they were not members of the local congregation. The Greek word translated stranger means, "sojourner." These men were faithful servants of God. In 2 Corinthians 3:1-2 we have an example of first-century evangelists carrying letters of recommendation with them as they traveled from place to place. In this way they could confirm their faithfulness and show others the charge they had received to travel throughout the world in order to evangelize.

What does it mean to send someone on his journey in a manner worthy of God? It means to provide for their immediate needs and also to provide funds for their travel expenses. Paul once asked the brethren in Rome to provide travel assistance for him so that he could travel to Spain for an evangelistic effort (Rom. 15:24).

The apostle John also commended Gaius for personally assisting the strangers. Jesus Himself set the precedent for financially supporting traveling evangelists when He sent His apostles out to preach the word (Matt. 10:5-15). Paul taught the brethren in Corinth to give financial support to preachers. He wrote, "The Lord commanded that those who proclaim the gospel should get their living by the gospel" (1 Cor. 9:14). Faithful brethren should provide for local evangelists who live among the congregation as well as those who travel from city to city with the financial support they need to do their work. Doing so is both a privilege and a duty. When we support them we become co-laborers of the good work they are doing.

A WARNING TO DIOTREPHES

> I have written something to the church, but Diotrephes, who likes to put himself first, does not acknowledge our authority. So if I come, I will bring up what he is doing, talking wicked nonsense against us. And not content with that, he refuses to welcome the brothers, and also stops those who want to and puts them out of the church.
>
> 3 John 1: 9-10

John had already written a letter to the church but evil Diotrephes refused to acknowledge his apostolic authority. I suspect he destroyed that epistle. Diotrephes liked to put himself first so that he could rule the congregation. As the "preeminent" person in the congregation, he refused to acknowledge the authority of an apostle of Jesus Christ. That is amazing until you read 2 Corinthians 12:11-12 and learn that some of the disciples in Corinth treated the apostle Paul with the same kind of disrespect.

There are two kinds of church leaders. There are some who force their own will upon the disciples and there are others who are humble servant leaders who seek to follow in the steps of Jesus and encourage the flock to follow them. Which is more Christ-like? Read Mark 10:35-45 to learn what Jesus had to say about leadership.

The King James Version says Diotrephes "loveth to have the preeminence among them." The Greek word "philoproteuo" means "to love to be first, hold the first place, or highest dignity." The root word is "proteuo." It means "to be first, hold the first place, or highest dignity." The root word only appears one time in Scripture and it is applied to Jesus Christ. "And he is the head of the body, the church. He is the beginning, the firstborn from the dead, that in everything he might be preeminent" (Col. 1:18).

God did *not* give preeminence to Diotrephes or to any other human being.

It was given to Jesus and to Jesus alone. Our Savior did not receive preeminence because of His love for position or power but because He obeyed God in all things. He was given preeminence and power after His death upon the cross (Phil. 2:9-11). After His resurrection Jesus said, "All authority in heaven and on earth has been given to me" (Matt. 28:18).

DIOTREPHES LOVED POWER: Diotrephes did not serve in order to mature the saints or to exalt Christ. He was a self-centered leader who served in order to become the most important person in the congregation. He served in order to exercise power over everyone else. Godly leaders seek to exalt Christ and they desire to help mature the saints (Eph. 4:11-16). Diotrephes' purpose was to enforce his own will upon the church. His leadership was distorted because he loved being first.

ACCEPT APOSTOLIC AUTHORITY: When John wrote to the church Diotrephes refused to accept his words of wisdom. He was quite different from the early disciples who "devoted themselves to the Apostle's teaching" (Acts 2:42). Diotrephes was devoted to his own authority. That is unacceptable behavior for a church leader! No man has the right to seek the authority that belongs only to Jesus Christ our Lord.

WICKED DEEDS: Diotrephes was an ungodly leader who spoke wicked nonsense against John and his faithful friends. More than that, he refused to welcome the traveling evangelists that came to the congregation for assistance. Diotrephes also stopped the brethren from helping them. Those who were bold enough to help these evangelists anyway were cast out of the church! It is probably safe to assume that Gaius was among those who were cast out by wicked Diotrephes.

John gave fair warning that he would take care of Diotrephes when he came to visit the church. Whether it is an apostle, an elder, an evangelist, or a church leader that is in error, faithful men must take a stand against their evil deeds. Paul spoke of a similar situation in 1 Timothy 1:19-20. "Some have made shipwreck of their faith, among whom are Hymenaeus and Alexander, whom I have handed over to Satan that they may learn not to blaspheme." John would surely exercise his apostolic authority against Diotrephes if he did not repent of his wrongdoing.

DEMETRIUS IS COMMENDED

> Beloved, do not imitate evil but imitate good. Whoever does good is from God; whoever does evil has not seen God. Demetrius has received a good testimony from everyone, and from the truth itself. We also add our testimony, and you know that our testimony is true.
>
> 3 John 1:11-12

In this passage good and evil are contrasted. It is imperative that we know the difference between the two. Do not "imitate evil but imitate good." Paul encouraged others to imitate him as he imitated Christ (1 Corinthians 11:1). It is likely, that in one way or another, we will imitate someone. That can be dangerous if we don't weigh the lifestyle of the person we imitate by the word of God.

Every good thing comes from God (James 1:16-17). Humans must learn to discern between what is good and what is evil. We are able to do this unless we allow our consciences to become seared as with a hot iron (1 Tim. 4:2). Some people refuse to believe the truth and will be sent a delusion from God that will cause them to believe a lie. Such people will be condemned (2 Thess. 2:8-12). We must know the difference between good and evil or we will choose incorrectly. Some people are naturally likeable but their lifestyle is contradictory to the Christian walk. Do not follow them! A lack of discernment will put our souls in grave danger. When we follow faithful believers we will be drawn closer to Christ.

Sometimes people imitate the ways of the world because it is the popular thing to do. There is absolutely no way to discern between what is wicked and what is good without an understanding of the word of God. We need to know the difference between good and evil. "Everyone who does good is from God; whoever does evil has not seen God." There are untold millions who living today who do not know the ways of God. Do not imitate them.

When we look at the lifestyle of Diotrephes we learn that he loved power and tried to dominate others. He was so determined to be preeminent that he ordered other believers to obey his will or they would be punished. The will of Diotrephes was not based upon scripture but on his desire for power.

Now we meet Demetrius, a man worthy of imitation. Without a doubt he followed that which was good. His fellow Christians saw the goodness in him and readily gave John a good report on his lifestyle. It is a wonderful privilege to inform people of the faithfulness and the goodness of believers who worship in other congregations.

Demetrius' faithfulness was confirmed by other believers and by the testimony of the apostle himself. We know the words of an apostle are reliable and true. Therefore, in one short verse we are privileged to meet a man whose goodness was confirmed from three reliable witnesses. Other Christians, John the apostle, and the truth itself bore witness to the goodness of Demetrius. All three testified to his Christian character. It will be wonderful to meet him and many other faithful servants of God when the Lord calls us home! As a believer, all we have the responsibility to refuse to imitate evil and to imitate good.

FINAL GREETINGS

> I had much to write to you, but I would rather not write with pen and ink. I hope to see you soon, and we will talk face to face. Peace be to you. The friends greet you. Greet the friends, each by name.
>
> 3 John 1:13-15

JOHN PROMISES TO VISIT SOON

John closes the epistle of 3 John with personal wishes to his friends. The word friend is "philos" in the Greek language. It means "loved one, beloved, dear, a friend." John hoped to make a personal visit *soon*! Did you notice the mention of pen and ink? Did you feel the urgency John felt to discuss their problems in more detail? While he had much to write, he preferred to make a personal visit to the congregation. He hoped to see them soon – face to face. Some problems cannot be solved without direct contact and, all too often, without some measure of confrontation.

The peace John mentions is from the word "shalom" in the Hebrew language and "eirene" in Greek. It was a common form of greeting for Israelites. Even today, many living in Palestine greet one another with the word "shalom." It was a common form of greeting among first-century Christians. We use the English word "hello." However, "shalom" is a much more meaningful greeting than our simple greeting of "hello." Greeting someone with the word "shalom" is more than just a greeting. It is a reminder of the peace (comfort of soul) bestowed upon the people of God. We know when we have peace but it is often beyond our human abilities to fully understand it.

Christian peace is the "peace of God that passes understanding" (Phil. 4:7). Jesus gives us a kind of peace that is different from that which is found in the world. Our Lord said, "Peace I leave with you, my peace I give to you. Not as the world gives do I give to you. Let not your hearts be troubled, neither let them be afraid" (John 14:27). Christian peace has everything to do with our hope in God and the assurance He gave us of eternal life.

Finally, John sent affectionate greetings from himself and his friends. This included the believers where John worshipped and those who were in Gaius' congregation. It would no doubt have encouraged Gaius when he received greetings from the friends. Gaius was also asked to extend the apostle's greetings to the friends where Gaius lived and to call them by name. The early Christians were more than just mere acquaintances. They were friends who loved each other and who knew each other by name. Is there anything more precious than to have someone to call you by name? These loving brethren were sharing an intimate greeting that was to be exchanged between both groups of believers.

With these few words the epistle of Third John is finished. It was written to address a very serious problem that was brought about by the actions of Diotrephes. However, the problem is overshadowed by the faithful service of Gaius and Demetrius – John's faithful friends. It was because of their example that I chose the theme for this epistle: RECEIVE FAITHFUL BRETHREN.

CLOSING REMARKS

FIRST JOHN: The epistle of 1 John has provided us with many important lessons. We learned about the Deity of Christ. We saw the need to walk in the light as He is in the light. We learned what it takes to conquer our sin problem. We learned about the coming of the antichrists. Their teaching was deceptive lies that proved to us that they were not of the apostles. We studied brotherly love and learned that without it we cannot love God. We also saw how love compels us to keep God's commandments. These truths and much more was brought to our attention through the epistle of 1 John.

SECOND JOHN: In 2 John we learned to stand against the false teaching of the antichrists. John presented the necessity for faithful brethren to discipline those who claim to teach the truth but are, in reality, teaching error. If we have fellowship with such people we become partakers with them of their evil works. Our silence makes us just as guilty of wrongdoing as those who were teaching falsehood.

THIRD JOHN: In 3 John we saw how the apostle gave comfort to faithful brethren such as Gaius and Demetrius while condemning unfaithful Diotrephes. The book also showed us the need to provide assistance to traveling evangelists as they go from place to place preaching the word. Third John concludes with greetings to the friends. Sharing greetings among friends is a nice way to end this study. Brethren should be friends.

It is hoped that *Love Letters from John* has deepened your understanding of the epistles of John. Keep on studying the word because doing so will cause your faith to grow. Remember daily the commandment to "love one another, for love is from God" (1 John 4:7).

DISCUSSION QUESTIONS:

1. Discuss the attitudes we should have toward our fellow disciples.
2. Discuss why we should give words of encouragement to those who have been treated unjustly by others.
3. List the four areas of encouragement John gave to Gaius.
4. Discuss the problems that were occurring in Gaius' congregation.
5. How does the preeminence of Jesus differ from that of Diotrephes? List the three actions that reveal the problem with Diotrephes.
6. Discuss the commendation of Demetrius.
7. Research the word "peace" and discuss how the peace Christ gives us is different than the peace that is given by the world (John 14:27).

Made in the USA
Charleston, SC
09 September 2016